"A beautiful and sensitive account of the lives and spirituality of the early Christian desert monastics. Chryssavgis' treatment of these strange, compelling figures is marked by an uncommon depth of understanding; under his discerning gaze, the world of the desert monastics comes alive for the reader. What really distinguishes his treatment, though, is his compassion for these ancient figures, his ability to meet them as fellow human beings who, like us, find themselves caught up in a mysterious and challenging spiritual journey."

—**Douglas Burton-Christie**, Loyola Marymount Univesity, and author of The Word in the Desert

"The resolute honesty of an Ed Abbey, the prophetic freedom of a Wallace Stegner, the profound love of a Charles de Foucauld—these were the qualities of the Desert Christians who thrived in Egypt and Palestine in the fourth, fifth, and sixth centuries. I've known for a long time that they are what I want to be when I grow up. This delightful book makes me more certain of that than ever. The sayings of Zosimas, here translated for the first time, are a wonderful addition to the English corpus of the Desert Christians.

"This is a spirituality for everyone who has ever gone through the desert (metaphorically at least), even if they've never lived in it like the early Christian monks. It reveals a practice that sings, a way of living that, as Abba Serapion said, 'makes us truly alive.'"

—**Belden Lane**, Professor of Theological Studies, Saint Louis University, and author of *The Solace of Fierce Landscapes*

"As scholarly astute as he is compassionate and wise, the author of *In the Heart of the Desert* truly illumines the very heart of the spirituality of the desert saints, a heart that, for all its rigorous asceticism, metaphysical transparency, and lofty attainment, is very much like our own in its brokenness, suffering, desolation, and struggle."

—**Vincent Rossi**, Director of Education for the American Exarchate of the Jerusalem Patriarchate of the Eastern Orthodox Church, and founder of the journal *Epiphany*

"The author succeeds in this masterful work in ways that others have not. He penetrates the spiritual/mystical/psychological depth of the desert contemplatives, the pioneer men and women who forged, through their lives, a vision of holiness in its contemplative dimension. He communicates the spirit of their supernatural, practical Christian humanism, which is always informed by humility, charity, and a keen discernment of human nature. Finally, he understands their commitment to a purified will, one empty of selfishness and grasping, and he is able to see them in the way they regarded one another."

> —**Wayne Teasdale**, author of *A Monk in the World: Cultivating a Spiritual Life*

"Here is a secret to living a rich spiritual life: When you need renewal, ideas, and inspiration, find whatever it is that takes you to your interior desert. If you don't know how to do this, read this excellent book."

> —**Thomas Moore**, author of *Care of the Soul: A Guide for Cultivating Depth* and *Sacredness in Everyday Life*

"The desert can be a fearful and imposing place without a guide, and Fr. Chryssavgis takes the reader through the rugged yet beautiful terrain of desert spirituality with clarity and empathy. The fathers and mothers of early Christian Egypt come alive in this fine study, with the added benefit of an original translation of the *Reflections* of Abba Zosimas. If I were to recommend a single book to introduce the spiritual riches of the desert—solitude, silence, humility, detachment, tears, and the encounter with the living God—this would be the book."

> —**Robert Fastiggi**, Sacred Heart Major Seminary

"In this book the Desert Fathers and Mothers show us how, surrounded as we are by a spiritual wasteland, we may yet make that desert bloom if we also dare to enter into the heart of its solitude."

> —**Louis Dupré**, Yale University, and editor of *Light from Light: An Anthology of Christian Mysticism*

"An invaluable guide to the teachings of the Desert Fathers and Mothers. John Chryssavgis eludicates the principles and practices of desert *metanoia* with exemplary sensitivity and depth. The love of God radiates from every page of this book; one cannot read it and come away unchanged."

> —**Philip Zaleski**, editor of *The Best Spiritual Writing* series, author of *The Recollected Heart* and *Gifts of the Spirit*, and senior editor of *Parabola* magazine

"'If you have a heart you can be saved,' says Abba Pambo. This is the very essence of the spirituality of the desert, and of Chryssavgis' presentation of these men and women, wrapped in a depth of silence, compassion, and ascetic simplicity. It will inspire people of all religious traditions."

—**Sir John Tavener**, composer and author

"An excellent introduction to the spiritual life based on the teachings of the Desert Fathers—as true today as they ever were and applicable to sincere seekers at all levels of spiritual commitment."

—**Rama Coomaraswamy**, author of *The Invocation of the Name of Jesus: As Practiced in the Western Church* and *The Destruction of the Christian Tradition*

"In this accessible volume Father Chryssavgis allows us to hear the voices of the Desert Fathers and Mothers in such a way that we too may drink from this eternal spring. Not the least attractive feature of the book is the illuminating commentary and sage counsel provided by Father Chryssavgis himself."

—**Harry Oldmeadow**, La Trobe University, Bendigo, and author of *A Christian Pilgrim in India: The Spiritual Journey of Swami Abhishiktananda (Henri Le Saux)*

"Chryssavgis has written a well-informed and sensitive study of the distinctive spirituality of abbas and ammas. 'When we [too] have addressed our demons,' he says, 'will we not also know the presence of angels in our life?. . . Our heart will beat in unison with the heart of the world.' This outstanding study also includes a complete translation of Abba Zosimas' *Reflections*."

—**Library Journal**

"*In the Heart of the Desert: The Spirituality of the Desert Fathers and Mothers* by Fr. John Chryssavgis surveys a treasury of ancient texts regarding Christianity, particularly those written by earliest Christian peoples who lived and survived in the desert as an act of Christian faith. Their exhortations, spiritual guidances, prayers, encounters with God, internal struggles, and testimonies have survived down the centuries, and here they are presented in an informative overview enhanced with extensive thought, wisdom, and meditation concerning the lives that worshiped God throughout the centuries. An especially welcome contribution to Christian studies and reference shelves, *In the Heart of the Desert* is a work of considerable scholarship and easily accessible by non-specialist readers."

—**Midwest Book Review**

# World Wisdom
# The Library of Perennial Philosophy

The Library of Perennial Philosophy is dedicated to the exposition of the timeless Truth underlying the diverse religions. This Truth, often referred to as the *Sophia Perennis*—or Perennial Wisdom—finds its expression in the revealed Scriptures as well as the writings of the great sages and the artistic creations of the traditional worlds.

*In the Heart of the Desert, Revised: The Spirituality of the Desert Fathers and Mothers* appears as one of our selections in the Treasures of the World's Religions series.

# Treasures of the World's Religions

This series of anthologies presents scriptures and the writings of the great spiritual authorities of the past on fundamental themes. Some titles are devoted to a single spiritual tradition, while others have a unifying topic that touches upon traditions from both the East and West, such as prayer and virtue. Some titles have a companion volume within the Perennial Philosophy series.

Cover: Monastery of the Syrians, Wadi al-Natrun, Egypt

# In the Heart of the Desert

*Revised*

## The Spirituality of the Desert Fathers and Mothers

With a translation of
Abba Zosimas' *Reflections*

J‍OHN C‍HRYSSAVGIS

*Foreword by*

The Most Reverend Metropolitan
Kallistos (Ware) of Diokleia

World Wisdom

In the Heart of the Desert, Revised:
The Spirituality of the Desert Fathers and Mothers
© 2008 World Wisdom, Inc.

Dr. John Chryssavgis is grateful to the Center of Theological Inquiry
at Princeton, which provided an oasis for the preparation of this book
during his sabbatical in the Spring of 2002.


World Wisdom and Dr. John Chryssavgis would like to thank Catherine Kostyn
for her kind assistance in creating of the index included in this book.

Back cover photograph by Melissa Lynch.

Most recent printing indicated by last digit below:

10 9 8 7 6 5 4


Library of Congress Cataloging-in-Publication Data

Chryssavgis, John.
  In the heart of the desert : the spirituality of the Desert Fathers and Mothers : with a
translation of Abba Zosimas' Reflections / John Chryssavgis ; foreword by The Most
Reverend Metropolitan Kallistos (Ware) of Diokleia. – Rev. ed.
    p. cm. – (Treasures of the world's religions) (The library of perennial philosophy)
  Includes bibliographical references and index.
  ISBN 978-1-933316-56-7 (pbk. : alk. paper)  1. Desert Fathers.  2. Spiritual life–
Christianity–History of doctrines–Early church, ca. 30-600.  I. Title.
  BR195.C5C47 2008
  270.2–dc22

                                                                                        2008015102

Printed in the United States of America on acid-free paper.

For information address World Wisdom, Inc.
P.O. Box 2682, Bloomington, Indiana 47402-2682

www.worldwisdom.com

*In the deserts of the heart*
*Let the healing fountain start.*

W.H. Auden (1907-1973)
*In Memory of W.B. Yeats*

*The road of cleansing goes through that desert.*
*It shall be named the way of holiness.*

Isaiah 35.8 (LXX)
*The Vision of Isaiah*

# Contents

# List of Color Illustrations

# List of Black-and-White Illustrations

"The father of Christian monasticism," Abba Antony the Great,
Greek icon, 16th century

# Publisher's Preface to the Original Edition

The words of spiritual counsel, which form the heart of this book, are as clear and timeless as the desert stars on a winter night. Not only do the sayings of the Desert Fathers possess the imprint of eternity, but the fresh and vital commentary by Father John Chryssavgis brings these ancient words into sharp focus; it brings them fully to life and provides a key which unlocks their relevance for the reader of today. This book is a well of wisdom from which anyone who finds himself in the desert of his own soul may drink freely from the water of life.

The desert may be understood on several different levels. The actual Egyptian desert to which these monks fled in the fourth and fifth centuries was, of course, an actual place. But the desert may also be understood as an inner geography of desolation and abandonment; it is the place, perhaps even in the midst of others, where we are most alone. It is the valley of our deepest solitude. Father John tells us that anyone who has experienced some aspect of deserted-ness, loneliness, brokenness, breakdown or break-up—whether emotionally, physically or socially—will connect with the profound humanity of the Desert Fathers and Mothers.

Various traditions from world religions teach that God enters into the empty soul. This is the meaning of *vacare Deo*. If in our prayers we long for His Presence and wait for Him with patience, confidence, humility and trust, then He will come into the center of our lives and establish there His kingdom. The universal and perennial message of these first Christian monks concerns the necessity of emptiness; the Fathers show us, by their examples, how to confront the chaotic impulses of the soul which drive us away from that still point where God is waiting. These are not only the demons confronted by Saint Antony; they are the demons which must be confronted in the arena of the soul by every man who seeks to rise above himself for the sake of God.

The Desert Fathers were spiritual combatants and their battlefield was the place where the forces of light engaged the forces of darkness in mortal struggle to control the destiny of the soul. This idea may seem antiquated to the modern reader; however, I would contend that every time we feel seriously conflicted, every disturbing thought which passes through our minds and which shocks and disappoints us, every time we feel that we have failed to be truly ourselves in the best sense, we are, at some level, engaged in the struggle of the desert. The harsh world of the Egyptian wilderness was the outward manifestation of that interior field of inner warfare. The mystery of the desert is discovered in this world below when we realize that the demons fight hardest when God is near; the darkness of the shadow is in direct proportion to the brilliance of the light.

The words of these Fathers and Mothers, sometimes inspiring and uplifting, sometimes agonizingly painful, sometimes humorous and sometimes full of sorrow, always speak straight from the soul. They have resonated through the centuries because they tell the story of the soul in its pilgrimage from darkness to light, from ignorance to truth, from sin to sanctity, from Egypt to the Promised Land. *In the Heart of the Desert* picks up the tale for today; it invites us to listen carefully with our hearts to the stories of these ancient monks. Regardless of our personal vision of the Absolute, each of us must participate in this story because, in the final analysis, it is the only story that is completely true.

Barry McDonald
World Wisdom
Bloomington, Indiana

# Foreword to the Revised Edition

In the life of each one of us, there are perhaps a few books—it may be very few indeed, no more than three or four—that have decisively altered our lives. After reading them only once, we are no longer the same; our imagination is suddenly enlarged, and we see ourselves and others with new eyes. For me, one such work is *The Desert Fathers* by Helen Waddell, which I read when I was sixteen. I bought it on a sudden impulse, not knowing what I would find inside its covers. At once my attention was caught and held by the stories of the Desert Fathers and Mothers which Deacon John Chryssavgis also presents to us so effectively in this present work. As I turned the pages of Helen Waddell's book, I said to myself: here is a world in many ways remote, even bizarre, and yet extraordinarily close to me, a world austere and yet profoundly compassionate, a world that at all costs I must learn more about when I grow older, a world that I must somehow make my own. Since then I have read many other studies on the monasticism of Egypt and Palestine, but scarcely any of them have conveyed to me the true meaning of Desert spirituality in the way that Deacon John has succeeded in doing.

Speaking of the stories and sayings of the Desert, Helen Waddell emphasizes their "timelessness." That also is the impression that they make on me. Precisely because the words of the Desert Fathers and Mothers are not systematic but intuitive, because they set before us not moral rules but living examples, their testimony is exceptionally direct, simple, and vivid. What strikes me above all is the unexpected sensitivity of these hermits and ascetics, their humility, their unwillingness to condemn, the generosity of their love. As Helen Waddell puts it, "The Desert has bred fanaticism and frenzy and fear: but it has also bred heroic gentleness. . . . Inhumanity to one's self had often its counterpart in an almost divine humanity towards one's neighbor."

This gentleness and humanity are well expressed in the description of Scetis, given in the late fourth-century text *The History of the Monks of Egypt*. Many of the stories to be found in the present book come precisely from the monastic settlements at Scetis:

> It is set in a vast desert, a day and a night's journey from the monasteries of Nitria, and it is reached by no path, nor is the track shown by any landmarks of earth, but one journeys by the signs and courses of the stars. Water is hard to find. . . . Here abide men perfect in holiness (for so terrible a place can be endured by none save those of absolute resolve and supreme constancy); yet is their chief concern the loving kindness that they show to one another and towards such as by chance reach that spot.

The quintessence of the Desert teaching is summed up in the answer given by Pimenion:

> A certain brother asked Abba Pimenion, saying, "What is faith?" And the old man said, "To live ever in loving kindness and in humbleness, and to do good to one's neighbor."

It is summed up equally in the words of an unnamed Desert Father:

> Devils do not cast out devils; but by gentleness you can call others back. For by such means as this does our God draw us to Himself.

When I think of Desert spirituality, I think at once of Bessarion's refusal to judge others:

> A brother, who had sinned, was turned out of the church by the priest. Abba Bessarion got up and went out with him, saying: "I too am a sinner."

The same sense of solidarity with others is movingly expressed in Abba Zosimas' petition, "Lord Jesus Christ, heal me through my brother's prayers."

Along with gentleness and humanity, the spirituality of the Desert is marked above all by a sense of God's immediate presence. For the desert-dwellers, God is very close; every stone in the wilderness breathes prayers. They regard prayer not as an occasional activity but as a dimension that enters into everything that they do:

"Pray without ceasing" (1 Thess. 5:17). Indeed, prayer for them is not so much something that they *do* but something that they *are*. So closely united was Abba Arsenios with his prayer that a brother, looking through the window of his cell, saw the old man "as if he were a single flame of fire." As Abba Joseph said, "If you really want, you can become all flame."

It is my hope and expectation that this book of Deacon John Chryssavgis, *In the Heart of the Desert*, will have upon contemporary readers something of the effect that *The Desert Fathers* of Helen Waddell had upon me nearly sixty years ago. Reading *In the Heart of the Desert*, I said to myself again and again: It is indeed so; it is exactly so. He shows how *The Sayings of the Desert Fathers* is, in his own words, "not a book of the past," but "a book of the age to come, or of a new age." He rightly speaks of the Egyptian hermits as "sparks of fire." May many who read the present book by Deacon John be set aflame by these living sparks.

+ Metropolitan Kallistos of Diokleia
February 2008

"The desert became a city,"
Monastery of the Archangel Gabriel, Fayoum, Egypt

# *Foreword to the Original Edition*

The first Christian monks lived nearly two thousand years ago but the accounts of their lives and the records of their words are still being read today. They were originally written down in Greek and Coptic but were soon translated into Latin, so that they could be read widely in all parts of Christendom.

It is perhaps surprising to find that such ancient texts are, like the Gospels, so fresh and available in this third millennium. It was a strange way of life, strange both to contemporary secular society in the fourth century and to other Christians at the time. These were men and women who chose to live outside the towns and villages of the ancient world, as far as possible from civilized life, often entirely alone. They had also chosen to be sexually alone for life; there were no children or lovers in the desert. They had very few possessions, and wanted to have as little as possible, choosing to do without them in order to be free for God. They lived in handmade huts or in caves, eating and drinking a sparse diet of bread and herbs with water. Their clothing was that of the poorest people, a simple garment, with a sheepskin that could be used as a blanket or rug. They were neither scholars nor preachers, neither teachers nor clerics, they came from all kinds of backgrounds but mainly from that of poverty and need. They learned how to be still and silent, to know themselves before God, waiting on the Lord, not helping others or interfering in their lives, but becoming themselves part of the redeeming work of Christ for the world.

Their behavior seemed as remarkable to their contemporaries then as it does now, whether the comments were favorable or hostile. These monks were people living on the edges, at the limits of both society and the church, and it seemed to some regrettable that as well as living without comfort and wealth, they had abandoned the duties and delights of ordered society to live apart from the treasures of a cultivated world, with no concern for education, literature, and the arts of the civilized man, with no involvement in corporate liturgical prayer, and no responsibility for the service of others in either the state or the church. On the other hand, many recognized in their lives a continuation of the eschatological attitudes of the early church, where Christians were aware of themselves as living in the last days, with no concern for the future on earth, eagerly awaiting the consummation of all things and therefore celibate and without children because the Child had been born and the orientation of the whole of life had changed. Many regarded the monks as heroes, seeing them as the successors of the martyrs, as those who followed most closely after the Savior. For these reasons, especially after the peace of the church under the Emperor Constantine, they attracted many tourists as well as serious seekers after God. Both of these approaches say more about contemporary society than about the monks.

Many read about or heard about this way of life and wanted to learn from it. They came to Egypt and to Palestine, and though many were moved and helped by the silence and solitude they found there, many of the assumptions and hopes of less perceptive contemporaries were contradicted by the actual approach to life of the monks and this could cause bewilderment and disappointment, until they realized what was at stake. Archbishop Theophilus of blessed memory once came with a certain judge to see Arsenius. The archbishop questioned Arsenius, wanting to hear some wisdom from him. For a while the hermit was silent, and then he replied, "If I tell you something, will you do it?" They promised that they would do it. So he said to them: "Wherever you hear Arsenius is, do not go there." Another time the archbishop wanted to see him, and sent a message first to ask if he would open the door to him. He sent a message back saying: "If you come here, I will open the door to you. But if I have opened the door to you, I must open it to all, and then I shall no longer be able to live here." When he heard this, the archbishop said: "Since my visit upsets him, I will not go to see to the holy man again" (Arsenius 7).

The visitors to the desert wanted to help the monks and their instinctive action was to offer them presents which would alleviate the severity of their life; but for the monks gifts were most unwel-come, being destructive of their choice of austerity and non-possession and again and again they refused what was offered. But the far more subtle assumption that they were there to give advice and counsel was for them a more dangerous trap which could have destroyed their whole way of life, making them not only no longer solitary and unknown but proud of themselves, the last temptation. They refused gifts, they abstained from either giving advice or working miracles, yet still people read about them and wanted to visit them. What continued to attract the attention of their contemporaries more than anything else was the sincerity of their lifestyle. They were genuinely doing what they claimed mattered to them. It is this strand of total self-commitment in practice to what is most deeply believed which accounts for their continued attraction through the centuries. They avoided teaching others, living their lives in the conviction that the only director of souls is God Himself.

Many of the sayings of the Desert Fathers and Mothers are unfinished, partial records of what was said, and all were subject to change. The later sources in Palestine laid greater stress, for instance, on giving teaching and advice; the monks who lived in communities spoke more about fraternal love within a group; the monks of the cities were more involved in works of charity, in learning and in corporate liturgical prayer. But the basic theme of implementing Christian baptism by total self-commitment for life in these hidden ways is found in them all and established a continuing tradition of solitary hermit life as well as creating the great monastic communities of East and West. In addition to the widespread monastic interest in this material from the desert, these sayings of the Desert Fathers and Mothers continue to give spiritual nourishment far beyond the cloister. They are a source which provides a foundation for praying and living, which is not limited by theological or national disputes and is not for a special kind of people, but for all.

In this volume, in addition to presenting the way of life and the chief concerns of the monks themselves (silence, humility, tears, the demons, charity and solitude), Dr. Chryssavgis has taken subjects of concern to contemporaries, such as ecology, gender and sexuality, and provided access to those sections of the ancient texts which will be of relevance for modern readers. Drawing on his deep knowledge of the area, he has chosen to present them in a way which shows his spiritual and pastoral concern, using the first person plural to involve the reader throughout. This book provides an accessible introduction to the sources themselves, with copious translations, a map, a time-line and bibliography. It also includes a translation into English of some material (The *Reflections* of Abba Zosimas), which has not been translated before.

This is material which has in it an air of eternity. As a later writer in this tradition put it:

> God is the life of all free beings. He is the salvation of all, of believers or unbelievers, of the just or the unjust, of the pious or the impious, of those freed from passions or those caught up in them, of monks or those living in the world, of the educated or the illiterate, of the healthy or the sick, of the young or of the very old. He is like the outpouring of the light, the glimpses of the sun, or the changes of the weather, which are the same for everyone without exception.

For almost two millennia these simple texts have continued to inspire people to follow the way of total commitment to God and this has often resulted in a life-style built on the same base as that of the lives of the Desert Fathers and Mothers, with realistic changes in detail caused by climate and education, as well as social and economic situation. Elsewhere these texts have been used by all sorts of people, from princes to paupers, for help towards their lives of prayer within society. As well as such strengthening of prayer for everyone, they have become part of the perennial search of humankind for beauty, by inspiring works of poetry, drama, music, opera and art. It is this perhaps that makes them so universally attractive and available today. What matters about them, in the long perspective of prayer, is not the details of their way of life but the fact that each day they lived out what they believed, convinced that "God was in Christ redeeming the world to Himself" and that no more was needed for salvation than the readiness to receive that truth. They are therefore still an encouragement and assurance for all in the present day. As Antony the Great said:

> Fear not goodness as something impossible nor the pursuit of it as something alien, set a great way off; it hangs only on our own

choice. For the sake of Greek learning, men go overseas, but the City of God has its foundations in every place of human habitation. The kingdom of God is within. Goodness is within us and it needs only the human heart.

Benedicta Ward SLG
Reader in the History of Christian Spirituality
Oxford University

"A spirituality that crosses cultures and borders,"
Monastery of the Syrians, Egypt

# INTRODUCTION

# Models of the Spiritual Way

There is a fourth century[1] Eucharistic prayer of Sarapion of Thmuis that expresses the center of the experience for the early Christians and of what their faith meant for them. The prayer addresses God:

We entreat you, make us truly alive.[2]

All of us know about the deeper longing to be truly alive. We have all felt the need to be more than "mere survivors" or "mere observers" in our world. Through the centuries people have had the same hope, the same dream. Sometimes these hopes and dreams were and are preserved inwardly, silently. At other times, they are proclaimed outwardly, publicly. Mostly, they are conveyed in stories and sayings, handed down over generations, allowing each of us to connect with their truths in personal, sometimes paradoxical ways. So, the more noble aspirations of human beings may be discerned everywhere; almost anywhere, at least, where people have lived and searched honestly.

If we are ready to search for such authentic human beings throughout history, then we shall sometimes discover them in unexpected places and in unconventional persons. One place, where men and women sought aggressively to understand the deeper meaning and the fuller measure of human existence, was the desert of early Christian Egypt. That dry desert, from the third century until around the end of the fourth century, became the laboratory for exploring hidden truths about Heaven and earth and a forging ground for drawing connections between the two. The hermits who lived in that desert tested and studied what it means to be human—

---

1. All dates referred to in this book are C.E. (in the Christian Era).
2. See J. Wordsworth, *Bishop Sarapion's Prayer-Book* (Hamden CT: Archon Books, 1964), p. 61. [My translation]

with all the tensions and temptations, all of the struggle beyond survival, all of the contacts with good and the conflicts with evil. And in the process, some of them made many mistakes; others made fewer mistakes. Whoever said that there is a clear and simple answer to the questions of life? Yet, these men and women dared to push the limits, to challenge the norms. Their questions and responses are to be found in collections of aphorisms—or "sayings," *Apophthegmata* (Ἀποφθέγματα), as they are called in the original Greek.

There is something else, moreover, that these "sayings" bring to light. The Fathers and Mothers who lived in the desert of Egypt remind us of the importance of story-telling, which we have for the most part forgotten in our age. Listening to their stories and sayings, meditating on them in silence and subsequently telling them to others, helped our ancestors to live humanely, to be more human, to remain truly alive. These stories and sayings were ways in which the desert elders themselves maintained a sense of continuity with their own past, while also fostering a sense of connection with future generations. Stories are a critical form of communication for people of all ages and all places. They were formative in ages of literacy and of illiteracy alike, transcending as they do barriers of age, education, social status and culture. Somewhere along the line, we lost our interest in, and our ability to hear, understand, and tell stories. Somewhere along the line, life became faster, and people grew less tolerant for that which comes only with time and with pain, with listening and with patience. The stories from the Egyptian desert are more than just a part of the Christian past. They are a part of our human heritage: they communicate eternal values, spiritual truths. Theirs is a silence of the deep heart and of intense prayer, a silence that cuts through centuries and cultures. We should stop to hear that heartbeat.

Sometimes, in fact, we shall need to stoop low in order to hear the sounds of their past. For, while they present us with models of the spiritual way, they do so in peculiar ways and with strange examples. In fact, these stories and sayings offer not simply models for imitation, but witnesses of a fullness and freedom to which we all aspire. These stories will indeed appear extreme in some ways, eccentric in other ways. The lifestyle of these desert dwellers was radical and in every way iconoclastic, smashing every understanding that we may have been brought up to imagine about finding ourselves and finding God. Nonetheless, they are at the same time, and for this very same reason, quite refreshing, entirely liberating.

For, although it may not be immediately evident to everyone how to connect with the words and ways of the desert, yet anyone who has experienced some aspect of deserted-ness, that is to say some form of loneliness, or else some form of brokenness, break-down or break-up—whether emotionally, physically, or socially—will be able to make the necessary connections. Each of us has known times of drought; dry and arid moments when we await refreshment and rain, when we wait for hope and life. Indeed, such experiences may comprise the very framework within which we are called to read and appreciate their words. It may not be true to desert spirituality or even fair to the desert elders themselves for us to consider their radical retreat and refreshing worldview through the lenses of suffering and woundedness. If this appears to diminish their uniqueness, then we would do well to remember that the Desert Fathers and Mothers might not at all have been surprised by this perspective. First, they expected people to approach them spontaneously—just as they *were*. And, second, they demanded that people open up to them sincerely—just as they *lived*. Our suffering and wounds have a remarkable way of unlocking the door to authenticity.

What is called for, then, is not a dry imitation of the behavior and ideals of the Desert Fathers and Mothers. Rather, an invitation is here extended to find the proper wavelength, that frequency where we are touched and transformed by their sayings. *The Sayings of the Desert Fathers*[3] is neither a biographical account of the lives of these hermits nor an historical record of their teachings. The notion of "objectivity" was not the primary concern of those who entered the Egyptian desert. Instead, the words of these Egyptian hermits resemble flashes of light; they are sparks of fire. And the reader should neither be overly impressed nor even be greatly dis-

---

3. Benedicta Ward, ed., *The Sayings of the Desert Fathers, The Alphabetical Collection* (Kalamazoo MI: Cistercian Publications, 1975). This book, the most accessible edition in the English language, serves almost exclusively as the basis for my remarks. I refer in the footnotes simply to the name of the elder and the number of the saying in this collection. I have, however, also frequently and significantly modified the translation from my own interpretation of the Greek original. See the bibliography (below) for further references and other collections.

tressed by their comments. Instead, the reader is supposed to catch alight, to catch afire. It is critical to remain open enough, to be sufficiently vulnerable to their austere yet suggestive counsel.

When visitors, whether hermits or lay persons, came to Egypt in order to meet one of these desert dwellers, invariably they would ask: "Give me a word, *abba*," or: "Speak a word, *amma*, how can I be saved," or again: "*Abba*, give me a way of life."[4] *Abba* is the Coptic word for father or elder; the Greek word was *geron* (γέρων). Alternatively, a visitor could seek the advice of an *amma* or spiritual mother. The fundamental context within which the words of the *abbas* and *ammas* were recorded in the past, and are perhaps also to be received in the present, is the relationship between the spiritual father or mother and the spiritual child or disciple. More will be said later on this relationship. However, for now we should think of these sayings as myth. Read them as powerful stories, each with an inner meaning or secret, a message or mask.

The aim is not imitation, but inspiration. We should resist the temptation to dismiss these elders as anachronistic; as well as the temptation to accept their words and world with a rosy romanticism. Behind these stories lies much more than certain historical figures who lived many centuries ago. Behind these sayings and stories is concealed the very face of God, Who speaks to each of us in the present and for all eternity. In a sense, *The Sayings of the Desert Fathers* is not a book of the past, of the fourth or fifth centuries. It may be described as a book of the age to come, or of a new age. They speak to our present age: of an experience of a new life, of a fullness of life, or of renewed life.

\*

\* \*

*The Sayings of the Desert Fathers* present us with the personal profiles of one hundred and twenty-seven *abbas* and three *ammas*. In all, there are 1202 sayings attributed to these elders. In the pages that follow, I shall be quoting generously from this text. The purpose of this book is to introduce readers to the world and thought of the early Desert Fathers and Mothers by allowing for informal conver-

---

4. *Sayings*, Sisoes 35; Antony 19; and Elias 8.

sations with some of their key representatives on the fundamental principles of their thought and lifestyle. I shall neither color nor endeavor to cover their statements in order to render them either more palatable or digestible. That would be unfair to them and untrue to their world, which was never intended to be generally entertaining or merely interesting. Rather, I shall allow these wise elders to speak for themselves, simply organizing their words in categories that might be more familiar to us today. This is why there will be an abundance of direct citations from the *Sayings* themselves. To understand the phenomenon of the desert, it is important to listen to those who lived their lives there; or rather, who renounced their lives in order to be present to that experience.

Although the content of this book is not intended to be narrowly academic, nonetheless its context is clearly scholarly, inviting the reader to pursue further references on the particular subjects raised. Substantial recent literary research, as well as increasing regional archaeological evidence, has been able to reconstruct numerous aspects of this phenomenon, providing scholars with religious, social, political, cultural, and artistic dimensions of this period in Christian history. We are, then, in a way perhaps not possible earlier, in a position to explore these sayings and encounter these elders quite vividly and personally.

This volume also presents, for the first time in the English language, a translation of a fifth-century text, the *Reflections* (*Dialogismoi*, Διαλογισμοί) of Abba Zosimas, which has played an important part in the development of the *Sayings* themselves, as we shall see below. The reflections are part and parcel of the same desert tradition, and so I have also incorporated them in my commentary on the spirituality of the Desert Fathers and Mothers.

If the background of this book (its flesh and bones) is scholarly, the intention (its heart) is unashamedly spiritual. For, if there are a number of profiles in the *Sayings*, they nevertheless essentially present us with one profile: the profile of what it means to be human. This picture will on occasion appear frightening to some readers. On other occasions, the same picture may appear comforting. It will, nevertheless, almost always be recognizable to each one of us. For this to happen, we need to sit silently with these *Sayings*. We must enter our own desert of stillness and retreat and pay close attention to the words and to the meanings behind these words. My purpose will not be to make the *Sayings* relevant to our time and ways; that often proves a futile exercise, which only distorts the original text and is an injustice both to it and to us. Rather, it will be to make our time and ways relate to the *Sayings*.

In so doing, I am reminded of the words of Abba Poemen:

Experience is a good thing; for, that is what tests a person.[5]

Abba Zosimas would say: "What power is contained in the words of the elders! Truly, whatever they said, they spoke out of experience and truth, as the sacred Antony also says.[6] Their words were powerful because they spoke of what they practiced, as one of the sages put it: 'May your life confirm your words!'"[7]

Abba Poemen also said: "Someone who teaches without doing what one teaches resembles a spring, which cleanses and gives drink to everyone else, but is not able to purify itself."[8]

The largest number of sayings is, in fact, attributed to this Abba Poemen. There are some two hundred and nine sayings under his name. The name "Poemen" is derived from the Greek word Ποιμήν meaning "shepherd," implying that most of the sayings may at first have been collected around this generic name.

Poemen further believes that teaching without doing, preaching without practicing, is an indication of hypocrisy.

A brother asked Abba Poemen: "What is a hypocrite?" The old man said to him: "A hypocrite is one who teaches one's neighbor something without making any effort to do it oneself."[9]

I am, however, at the same time comforted by yet another saying of this compassionate elder:

A brother said to Abba Poemen: "If I give my brother a little bread or something else, what happens when the demons spoil these gifts by telling me that it was only done in order to please people?" The old man said to him: "Even if it is done to please people, we are still

---

5. Poemen 24.

6. Abba Zosimas, *Reflections* XIV, a. See also Athanasius, *Life of Antony* (New York: Paulist Press, 1980), ch. 39.

7. *Reflections* XIV, a. See also John Moschus, *Spiritual Meadow*, ch. 219, pp. 194-195 (*Patrologia Graeca* [PG] 87: 3109-3112).

8. Poemen 25.

9. Poemen 117.

obliged to offer what we can." He told him the following parable. "Two farmers lived in the same town. One of them sowed and reaped only a small and poor crop, while the other did not even trouble to sow and reaped absolutely nothing. If a famine comes upon them, which of the two will find something to live on?" The brother replied: "The one who reaped the small poor crop." The old man said to him: "So it is with us: we sow a little poor grain, so that we will not die of hunger."[10]

This book is written in an effort to sow even a little poor crop!

10. Poemen 51.

# O N E

# *The Text through the Centuries*

Reading through *The Sayings of the Desert Fathers*, one has a sense of the rough, arid geography that surrounded these elders. Their words are dry and disconnected, almost incomprehensible outside the historical and spiritual context that gave birth to them. This is also one of the reasons why the *Sayings* defy precise dating. However, if we cannot speak of actual dates, we are able to refer to literary development. It may be helpful in this regard to speak of three significant stages in the development of these *Sayings*, to which we might also add a fourth.

The first stage is *the transmission of these sayings* or aphorisms to visitors who approached the elders in the desert. The *Sayings* is a literature that emerged in the early fourth century among the desert ascetics of Egypt, Syria and Palestine. Originally, they were a verbal tradition—they were precisely that: sayings! Moreover, they were initially transmitted in Coptic, Greek, Syriac and Latin. People would travel far and wide to reach these desert dwellers in order to seek their advice and prayers. Therefore, the sayings became the spontaneous words relating to impressive deeds of these elders, recorded for purposes of edification and emulation, remembered from generation to generation and from disciple to disciple.

The second stage is *the transition of the elders' sayings from an oral to a written tradition.* This development occurs somewhere toward the end of the fourth and, probably, the early fifth centuries. During this stage, the sayings tend to lose some of their spontaneity and become a little more static. We begin to lose sight of the personal element that sparked these words. More especially, the process and the struggle that originally shaped these words are also concealed. Furthermore, although most of the monks and nuns were Copts—native Egyptians—their sayings are for the most part preserved in Greek.[1]

A third stage involves *the development of these sayings* from the level of mere transliteration to that of edited written transmission. This occurs toward the middle of the fifth century, when several collections of sayings begin to appear. Apart from the alphabetical collection (which serve as the basis for our reflections here) there also appear anonymous collections, systematic collections (organized under headings such as prayer, humility, obedience etc.), and even numerous local collections. This is the stage of collection, of correction, and of copying. It is the period of rearrangement and revision, with little or no emphasis on modern assumptions of accuracy or fidelity. The "objective truth" that always matters, is the life-giving relationship between an elder and a disciple.

A final stage that should be added to the above three is the long period that separates us from the *Sayings*. Some 1500 years later, we live in a very different world and speak a very different language. The Desert Fathers and Mothers had no access to "quick fix" solutions or many modern technical resources; they did not know sugar or aspirin; they had no eyeglasses or false teeth; and they were limited in their reading material—after all, how many books could you take with you to the desert? Birth and death were not medical or hospital affairs; and travel was difficult and dangerous. If they spoke of a journey or a way, there were particular connotations implied. Their world was small, though it would have felt huge; and its center was somewhere in the Mediterranean. The earth too was the center of the universe. Even their understanding of monasticism differed from ours. In their time, monastic representatives were organized in a loose and flexible manner, allowing for little contact with the outside world and even less availability of information.

Yet, in their time, people visited Egypt from all over the world. Travelers would especially journey from Palestine to Egypt in order to visit these simple elders of the desert. From as early as the mid-fourth century, some of the better-known pilgrims include Jerome

---

1. For further insights into this and the next stages of the development, see the introduction (below) to Abba Zosimas' *Reflections*.

and Rufinus, Palladius and Evagrius, as well as John Cassian[2] who later translated this monastic tradition for the West.

Toward the end of the fourth century, a movement also began in the opposite direction, from Egypt to Palestine. Three hundred monks left Egypt definitively for Sinai, Jerusalem and the region around the Dead Sea, some of them even traveling as far as Asia Minor. From the year 380 onwards, and especially from the turn of the fifth century, the desert dwellers of Egypt also directed their steps to the region near Gaza, known both for its fertility and its solitude.

The deciding factors for this massive monastic emigration seem to include, on the more personal and religious planes, the deaths of the two Macarii—of the Egyptian in 390, and of the Alexandrian in 393—and, on the more political and social planes, the persecution of intellectualists and Origenists following their condemnation by Theophilus of Alexandria in 399.[3] The first generation of desert dwellers had come to a close, and their monastic successors began to seek new places to set root.

At some time between 380 and 400, Abba Silvanus, a Palestinian by birth and one of the more renowned elders of the Egyptian desert, moved with his twelve disciples briefly to Sinai and, finally, to Palestine. In Scetis, the Abba lived with his disciples in the semi-eremitic manner,[4] with scattered cells around his own dwelling and a central church for worship on Saturday and Sunday. The same lifestyle was adopted near Gerara, in Palestine, where the group later settled.

In fact, the scenic section along the Mediterranean Sea, between Thavatha, Maiouma and Ascalon, near the well-known region of Gaza, quickly became a strategic crossroad for those coming from north and south in search of God "in deserts and mountains, and in caves and holes in the ground" (Heb. 11.38). On

2. About Cassian, we are informed in this very collection of *Sayings*, Cassian 1. On the collections of the *Sayings*, see C. Stewart, *The World of the Desert Fathers* (Oxford: Fairacres Press, 1986). On the development from an oral to a written culture, see also P. Rousseau, *Ascetics, Authority, and the Church* (Oxford: Oxford University Press, 1978), especially pp. 68-76.

3. This Theophilus is mentioned in the *Sayings* (see the section on "Detachment" below).

4. See below, Section ii on "The Age of the Desert Fathers and Mothers."

account of its privileged position—in terms of geography, climate, and history—Palestine was to prove a remarkable place of welcome and continuity for Christian monasticism toward the end of the fourth century. Its accessibility by sea and land, its proximity to Egypt, Syria and the Holy Land, and its prominence in Hellenistic and Roman times, allowed the Palestinian region around Gaza to provide a critical haven for particular expressions of monasticism, offering fresh Christian perspectives in the spiritual and intellectual tradition of the monastic phenomenon.

\*
\* \*

Why, then, is it that these *Sayings of the Desert Fathers* still exercise—as indeed they have done throughout the centuries—considerable influence and attraction on people who read them? Augustine of Hippo read Athanasius' account of Antony and was "set on fire" by it.[5] For Abba Zosimas, the *Sayings* were the very air that he breathed.

> The blessed Zosimas always loved to read these *Sayings of the Holy Fathers* all the time; they were almost like the air that he breathed. It is from these *Sayings* that he came to receive the fruit of every virtue.[6]

Certainly, there has, in recent years, been a plethora of publications—both academic and popular—relating to the words and wisdom of these *abbas* and *ammas*.[7] Perhaps it is because of the commitment of these hermits. Perhaps it is because of their inner conviction. Perhaps their spirituality was appreciated as "earthly," not too speculative or abstract. Certainly their sayings are surprising in many ways; even shocking in some other ways. I believe that the

---

5. *Saint Augustine: Confessions*, ed. H. Chadwick (Oxford: Oxford University Press, 1991), Book VIII, vi, 15 (p.143). Cf. also VIII, xii, 29 (p.153).

6. Abba Zosimas, *Reflections* XII, b.

7. See, for example, H. Nouwen, *The Way of the Heart: Desert Spirituality and Contemporary Ministry* (New York: Seabury Press, 1981); R. Bondi, *To Pray and to Love: Conversations on Prayer with the Early Church* (Minneapolis: Fortress Press, 1991); B. Lane, *The Solace of Fierce Landscapes: Exploring Mountain and Desert Spirituality* (Oxford, 1998); A. Gruen, *Heaven Begins Within You: Wisdom from the Desert Fathers* (New York: Crossroad, 1999). A more complete list of sources on desert thought and spirituality may be found in the bibliography below.

words of these elders smash the structures of complexity and rationalization with which we often clutter and confuse our lives. Their lives somehow seem to locate pockets of deadness in our lives, enabling us to become truly alive. What they are in fact saying to us most of the time is quite simply: be what you are called to be!

> One of the fathers asked Abba Nistheros the Great, the friend of Abba Antony: "What good work should I be doing?" He said to him: "Are not all actions equal? Scripture says that Abraham was hospitable, and God was with him. David was humble, and God was with him. Elias loved interior peace, and God was with him. So, *do whatever you see that your soul desires according to God,* and guard your heart."[8]

8. Nistheros 1.

# T W O

# *The Age of the Desert Fathers and Mothers*

Christian monasticism began on a Sunday morning in the year 270 or 271 in a small Egyptian village. The Gospel passage read in worship that day included the words:

> If you want to be perfect, go, sell your possessions and give to the poor, and you will have treasure in heaven. Then come, follow me. (Matt. 19.21)

In the congregation, there sat a young man called Antony who, on hearing these words, sought a life not merely of relative poverty but of radical solitude. Antony's step into the uninhabitable and inhospitable desert was little noticed outside, or indeed even inside, his village at the time. Nevertheless, when he died at the age of 106,[1] his friend and biographer Athanasius of Alexandria informs us that the "desert had become a city,"[2] meaning that thousands had regularly flocked to Antony to be taught by him and had made the desert their home. Antony of Egypt was to become known as the father and founder of desert monasticism.

In Egypt, there were three main types of monasticism that developed, roughly corresponding to three geographical locations:

a) *The hermit life*, found in lower Egypt, where Antony himself became the model. Here monks lived an isolated and austere life.

b) *The cenobitic or communal form*, found in upper Egypt, where Pachomius formed several communities of monks and of nuns, who prayed and worked together.

---

1. See J. Lawyer, "St. Antony of Egypt and the Spirituality of Aging," in *Cistercian Studies Quarterly* 35, 1 (2000): 55-74, where the author speaks of "successful ageing."

2. *Life of Antony*, ch. 14. In fact, monasticism did not "begin" in Egypt but in the divine inspiration of several personalities throughout the early Christian world. Evidence points toward desert asceticism as appearing simultaneously and independently in numerous regions of the empire, such as Egypt and Syria.

c) And, *the middle way*, found in Nitria and Scetis, west of the mouth of the Nile River, started by Ammoun. This is known as *the semi-eremitic or the semi-cenobitic way.* Here a loosely knit group of settlements, comprising of two to six monastics, looked to and lived with a common spiritual elder. On Saturdays and Sundays, a number of these small monastic families would also worship together. It is primarily among representatives of this third form of monasticism that our collection of *The Sayings of the Desert Fathers* appears.

Antony lived in a time of crisis and transition. For three hundred years it had been a risk to be baptized into Christianity; adherents to this faith were considered outcasts and ostracized by the very fact of their conversion. In fact, with the edict of persecution in 303, Antony left his desert retreat for the first time, and visited Alexandria where he expected to be martyred. The aim of the Christian life, after all, was always to be prepared to die a martyr for Christ; or, at the very least, to live a life of continual sacrifice. Antony was not in fact martyred during this excursion and returned to his desert retreat. Just a matter of ten years later, with the edict of toleration issued in 313, Antony entered the "inner mountain," as he liked to call the place of deeper solitude. At a time when the rest of the Empire began to relax its stringent attitudes toward Christians, Antony began to intensify his ascetic discipline.

Historians have often referred to Antony as a revolutionary. Yet, in a sense, Antony was not innovating by moving out into the desert. The rest of the Church was in fact opening up a new chapter in its history. The Christian Church was beginning a new relationship with the authorities of this world, with the Empire of Rome. Coincidentally, but perhaps not accidentally, Antony increased his ascetic labors just as the rest of his brothers and sisters in the Christian church were relieved of the threat of persecution, which was ever present during the first three centuries. He considered his monastic ascetic labors as interchangeable with the martyr's ultimate sacrifice. Antony was in fact nostalgic for the spirit of martyrdom, which had nurtured the Church for three centuries. It was, by around the year 300, no longer a risk to be a Christian. Indeed, Christianity was soon to become the formal religion of the empire. Numbers of those baptized rose dramatically; standards dropped drastically. The Church began to compromise between "the things of God and the things of Caesar" (cf. Luke 20.25). The voice of the desert's heart replaced the voice of the martyr's blood. And the Desert Fathers and Mothers became witnesses of another way, another age, another kingdom.[3]

The hermits who sought refuge in the desert of Egypt reminded the rest of the church that "here we have no lasting city, but we are looking for the city that is to come" (Heb. 13.14). In so doing, they founded an alternative Christian society. This probably occurred unintentionally on their part. Nevertheless, their influence lasted long after their time. They promoted a way of life that reflects a reversal of all ordinary social values and expectations.

Society expects its citizens to be active and productive. In society, you are useless if you are not valuable. This expectation translates today into our attitudes toward minorities, or toward the elderly, the disabled, and especially young children. The Desert Fathers and Mothers proclaimed a different set of values, where change occurs through silence and not war; where inaction may be the most powerful source of action; and where productivity may be measured by obscurity, even invisibility. The same values were seen in a new perspective, with new dimensions. The desert elders looked for the roots of our attitudes and actions as human beings. They searched for the spiritual roots of our life. If we are to consider Antony as being radical, then it may be helpful to remember that the word "radical" is derived from the Latin term that implies a search for "roots."

When Athanasius wrote his *Life of Antony,* just a year after the hermit's death in 356, he was certainly doing something quite radical. In his age, it was fashionable to write the biography of someone important. Yet, importance was normally judged by such criteria as one's noble status, one's financial affluence or familial influence. What mattered most was one's secular authority or social outreach. By placing Antony's biography alongside those of famous emperors and governors, Athanasius was conveying a clear message. He was reminding the people of his time, as well as of ours, that the spiri-

---

3. In fact, the Greek term for martyr (*martys,* μάρτυς) is the same word for witness (*martyria,* μαρτυρία). Origen of Alexandria regarded the ascetic way as "a martyrdom of conscience." See his treatise *Exhortation to Martyrdom* (New York: Paulist Press, 1979); see also Eusebius of Caesarea, *Church History,* Book VI, 3.

tuality of the Desert Fathers and Mothers was indeed revolutionary. Theirs was a change that was out of sight, unrecorded in history books. Yet, it was a change that proved cataclysmic, recorded silently in human hearts. It was a protest against the complacency of the Christian world. Athanasius was informing his readers that the desert tested the readiness of these elders to live, even to die for God. The desert was what ultimately kept alive the fiery spirit of the martyrs. The words, then, of these desert elders are more than mere sayings; they are a profound statement.

# Some of the Key Personalities

We have already briefly looked at Antony of Egypt and we shall return to his sayings throughout this book. He is perhaps the best known of the early monastics, but was probably neither the first nor was he the foremost monk of his time. Monasticism seemed to develop contemporaneously, and indeed quite independently, in many parts of the early Christian world. Elsewhere, however, there was no other hermit, whose actions and words caught the attention of the early world—at least not in the way that Athanasius describes Antony. And yet there were many others, men and women, who shaped even the *Sayings* themselves.[1] In this section, we shall offer brief insights—literally, biographical snapshots—into the lives of five of these, including one Desert Mother.

## Abba Arsenius

We have, in the *Sayings*, a fairly detailed biographical sketch of Arsenius. There is information about his past and background in Asia Minor; his practices and teaching in Egypt; and even of his friends and acquaintances in both these places, where he was clearly well-known.

> Abba Daniel [one of his disciples] used to say this about Abba Arsenius: "His appearance was angelic, like that of Jacob. His body was graceful and slender, his long beard reaching down to his waist. Through much weeping, his eyelashes had fallen out. Tall of stature, he was bent with old age. He was ninety-five when he died. For forty years he was employed in the palace of Theodosius the Great, who was the father of Arcadius and Honorius. Then he lived

---

1. For useful introductions to the Desert Fathers and Mothers, see. S. Ramfos, *Like a Pelican in the Wilderness: Reflections on the Sayings of the Desert Fathers* (Brookline: Holy Cross Press, 2000); and L. Swan, *The Forgotten Desert Mothers: Sayings, Lives, and Stories of Early Christian Women* (Mahwah NJ: Paulist Press, 2001).

for forty years in Scetis, ten years at Troe above Babylon, opposite Memphis, and three years at Canopus of Alexandria. The last two years he returned to Troe where he died, finishing his course in peace and fear of God. He was a good man, 'filled with the Holy Spirit and faith' (Acts 11.24). He left me his leather tunic, his white hair shirt and his palm-leaf sandals. Although unworthy, I wear them, in order to gain his blessing."[2]

We know, for example, that Arsenius abandoned a life of palatial wealth and comfortable style.

> While still living in the palace, Abba Arsenius prayed to God in these words: "Lord, lead me in the way of salvation." And a voice came saying to him: "Arsenius, flee from people and you will be saved."[3]

Born in Rome around 354, Arsenius was well educated and of senatorial rank. He was appointed by the Emperor Theodosius to tutor the two princes, Arcadius and Honorius. Clearly, he sacrificed a great deal when he left for Egypt. He traveled by sea to Alexandria in 394, already at a mature age, and from there visited Scetis where he became the disciple of one of the more colorful figures of the Egyptian desert, Abba John the Dwarf. Later, he assumed the life of a hermit, attracting three disciples of his own. He was renowned for his austere ascetic practices, and especially his extreme silence. He died around 449. Forty-four sayings are preserved under his name, but others have also reached us through the stories of certain desert elders.

Arsenius is perhaps *the one elder who seems to combine all of the virtues of the desert*: ascetic struggle, spiritual detachment, prayer and tears. These are concepts that we shall examine more carefully later. Yet, for now, we can just imagine the forbidding combination, in Arsenius' personality, of the fine education in his early years and the strict solitude in his later years; of his former wealth and current poverty. The simple ascetics in the desert must have been in awe of Arsenius' spiritual nobility.

> It was said of Abba Arsenius that, just as none in the palace had worn more splendid garments than when he lived there, so no one in the church wore such poor clothing as he.[4]

2. Arsenius 42.
3. Arsenius 1.
4. Arsenius 4.

One day Abba Arsenius consulted an old Egyptian monk about his own thoughts. Someone noticed this and said to him: "Abba Arsenius, how is it that you with such good education in Latin and Greek, ask this peasant about your thoughts?" He replied: "I have indeed been taught Latin and Greek, but I do not know even the alphabet of this peasant."[5]

Indeed, the humility of Arsenius was perhaps more overwhelming than his achievements.

It happened that, when Abba Arsenius was sitting in his cell, he was harassed by the demons. His servants, on their return, stood outside his cell and heard him praying to God in these words: "God, do not leave me. I have done nothing good in Your sight. But according to Your Goodness, let me now at least make a beginning of doing good."[6]

Arsenius may always have regarded himself as a beginner, but his colleagues saw him as advanced in the ways of the desert.

It was said of Abba Arsenius that on Saturday evenings, preparing for the glory of the Sunday, he would turn his back on the sun and stretch out his hands in prayer toward the heavens, until once again the sun shone on his face. Then he would sit down.[7]

Yet, if he was strict on himself, he was always generous and compassionate in the advice that he offered to others.

Abba Mark [another of his disciples] asked Abba Arsenius: "Is it good to have nothing extra in the cell? I know a brother who used to have some vegetables and he has pulled them up." Abba Arsenius replied: "Undoubtedly that is good, but it must be done according to one's ability. For, if one does not have the strength for such a practice, then one will soon plant others."[8]

Abba Daniel used to tell how when Abba Arsenius learned that all the varieties of fruit were ripe, he would say: "Bring me some." He would taste a very little of each, just once, giving thanks to God.[9]

---

5. Arsenius 6.
6. Arsenius 3.
7. Arsenius 30.
8. Arsenius 22.
9. Arsenius 19.

In his own teaching to others, Arsenius placed a great deal of emphasis on two things: on thanksgiving to God and on personal willingness.

> Once, at Scetis, Abba Arsenius was ill and he was without even a scrap of linen. As he had nothing with which to buy any, he received some through another's charity and he said: "I give you thanks, Lord, for having considered me worthy to receive this charity in your name."[10]
>
> A brother questioned Abba Arsenius in order to hear a word from him, and the old man said to him: "Strive with all your might to bring your interior activity into accord with God."[11]
>
> He also said: "If we seek God, He will show Himself to us; and if we keep Him, then He will remain close to us."[12]

## Abba Poemen

Poemen is *the quintessential Desert Father*. His name, as we have already seen, may imply that the first kernel of sayings was either directly attributed to him or else at least assembled in his honor. In spite of disputes about the existence of more than one Egyptian elder by this name, Poemen's sayings quite possibly constitute the nucleus out of which the entire literature developed. Almost one-seventh of the complete alphabetical collection comprises sayings by Poemen. There are one hundred and eighty-seven *apophthegmata* in the original edition, and another twenty-two discovered more recently. Abba Poemen also figures in a number of other sayings throughout the collection. Just as Arsenius personifies the desert truths, Poemen's sayings and stories embrace, in both their quality and their quantity, the entire range of monastic values and virtues.

Poemen's personal connections were with such monks as John the Dwarf, Abba Agathon, and Abba Moses. He probably outlived Arsenius, possibly leaving Scetis toward the end of the fourth century with his seven disciples and settling in Terenuthis where he

10. Arsenius 20.
11. Arsenius 9.
12. Arsenius 10.

died around 449. His sayings refer to a number of close relatives, such as: brothers, mother, nephew, and even reference to a child. Unlike their more severe counterparts in places such as Syria, many Egyptian monks retained ties with family. This may be why Poemen emphasized the importance of not tolerating unfinished business. He understood well the risks involved in leaving personal or familial matters unresolved.

> While he was still young, Abba Poemen went out one day to an old man in order to ask him about three thoughts. Having reached the old man, he forgot one of the three thoughts and returned to his cell. But as he was stretching out his hand to turn the key, he remembered the thought, which he had forgotten, and leaving the key, he returned to the old man. The old man said to him: "You have come quickly, brother." He replied: "At the moment when I was putting out my hand to grasp the key, I remembered the thought which I was trying to find; so I did not open the door, but have retraced my steps." Now the length of the way was very great, and the old man said to him: "Poemen, shepherd of the flock, your name will be known throughout Egypt."[13]

For Poemen, what belongs and binds us to the past or indeed even to the future also renders us unable to live in the present.

> Abba Poemen was asked for whom this saying was appropriate: "Do not be anxious about tomorrow" (Matt. 6.34). The old man said: "It is said for the person who is tempted and has little strength, so that such a person may not worry, saying within: 'How long must I suffer this temptation?' That person should rather say each day: 'Just today.'"[14]

Even details mattered to Poemen. He believed that there was a clear series of stages in the battle against evil.

> The old man said: "Passions work in four stages—first, in the heart; secondly, on the face; thirdly, in words; and fourthly, it is always essential not to render evil for evil in deeds. If you can purify your heart, passion will not reveal itself in your expression; but if it reaches your face, then take care not to speak; and if you do speak, at least cut the conversation short in case you do render evil for evil."[15]

13. Poemen 1.
14. Poemen 126.
15. Poemen 34. Abba Zosimas speaks of a tapestry of thoughts that are "weaved": see *Reflections* III, b; IV, d; V, i, b; and VI, b.

We have become so familiar with Freud's stages of sexual development, with Piaget's stages of cognitive development, with Erikson's stages of personal maturation, and even perhaps with Fowler's stages of religious faith. Should we not also pay closer attention to the significance of the spiritual stages of our inner development? The desert elders recognize the stages of the spirit. They know that these are not random, but developmental. Moreover, they know them to the smallest detail, appreciating the various gradations within each stage, the particular shades within each gradation, and even the integration of each of these. What we miss in the spiritual sphere is so tangible for them; it is real in their experience. They would bump into realities shaped by the spiritual laws of the heart in much the same way as we would collide into a wall or a table because of the physical laws of nature.

These "laws" are there; it is just that we miss them. They are within our grasp, but for some reason they are not within our sight.

> Abba Poemen also said: "The wickedness of people is hidden behind their back."[16]

This means that it is easy for particular aspects of our life to remain hidden. It is a temptation to cheat. It is always tempting to speak in one way and to act in another. Yet, the aim in the spiritual life is constantly to draw together the diverse elements that comprise our life.

> Abba Poemen said: "Teach your mouth to say that which you have in your heart."[17]

We are called to examine and strengthen every aspect of our life, and not simply to focus on one or another facet.

> A brother asked Abba Poemen: "Can a person be confident in achieving one single work?" The old man said to him that Abba John the Dwarf said: "I would rather have a little of all the virtues."[18]

Abba Zosimas is in agreement:

> The blessed Abba Zosimas also used to say: "Once someone told me: 'Abba, the commandments are numerous and the intellect is

16. Poemen 121.
17. Poemen 63.
18. Poemen 46.

darkened in considering which ones to keep and which ones not to keep.' I responded: 'This should not trouble you. Rather, consider the following. When you are unattached to things, then you easily acquire virtue. And when you do not seek after them, you will not be mindful of wrong done to you.'"[19]

Indeed, the custom in the desert was to defer to the wisdom of the past, to conform to a philosophy that sought to incorporate an entire lifestyle. Abba John had even recommended the following detailed advice:

> Abba John said: "I think it best for a person to have a little bit of all the virtues. Therefore, get up early every day and acquire the beginning of every virtue and every commandment of God. Use great patience, with fear and long-suffering, in the love of God, with all the fervor of your soul and body. Exercise great humility, bear with interior distress; be vigilant and pray often with reverence and groaning, with purity of speech and control your eyes. When you are despised, do not get angry; be at peace, and do not render evil for evil. Do not pay attention to the faults of others, and do not try to compare yourself with others, knowing that you are less than every created thing. Renounce everything material and that which is of the flesh. Live by the cross, in spiritual warfare, in spiritual poverty, in voluntary spiritual asceticism, in fasting, penitence and tears, in discernment, in purity of soul, taking hold of that which is good. Do your work in peace. Persevere in keeping vigil, in hunger and thirst, in cold and nakedness, and in sufferings. Shut yourself in a tomb as though you were already dead, so that at all times you will think that death is near."[20]

John's words appear to be beyond most of us. But Poemen is quick to add:

> We do not need anything except a vigilant spirit.[21]

Poemen seems not to have been as radically demanding on others as, for instance, Abba Sisoes:

> A brother asked Abba Sisoes: "Can a person keep all the thoughts in control, without surrendering any to the evil one?" And Abba Sisoes said to him: "It is true that there are some who give nothing to the enemy."

19. *Reflections* VII, a.
20. John the Dwarf 34.
21. Poemen 135.

The same brother put the same question to Abba Poemen who said to him: "There are some who receive ten and give one."[22]

We are, says Poemen, to do the best that we can—no more, but also no less! The result is that we can never be critical of, or even correct, another person. This is where renouncing the past and recognizing the present merge in the virtue of love.

Some of the fathers questioned Abba Poemen saying: "If we see a brother in the act of committing a sin, do you think that we ought to reprove him?" The old man said to them: "For my part, if I have to go out and see someone committing a sin, I pass on my way without reproving him."[23]

Abba Poemen also said: "Instructing your neighbor is the same thing as reproving your neighbor."[24]

Such an attitude gave Poemen the spiritual space and sense of freedom that characterizes his entire teaching.

A brother asked Abba Poemen: "Is it better to speak or to be silent?" The old man said to him: "The person who speaks for God's sake does well; and the person who keeps silent for God's sake also does well."[25]

Our actions and words matter less for Poemen; what matter most are our inner disposition and emotion.

## Abba Macarius of Egypt

Macarius the Great was born around the year 300 in Egypt. His worldly profession was as a camel-driver and trader. He was an ordained priest and one of the founders of monasticism in Scetis, where he moved after being falsely accused—in fact, he voluntarily accepted the accusation, although he was later cleared because he was not involved at all—for the pregnancy of a young girl. Like many of the early monks in Egypt, he traveled around, not remaining fixed in one place for too long. Macarius was deeply influenced by Antony the Great, whom he visited twice. He died in

22. Poemen 89 and 88.
23. Pomen 113.
24. Poemen 157.
25. Poemen 147.

the year 390. Forty-one sayings have been preserved under Macarius' name, together with certain other sayings, which are found in the stories of other elders.

Abba Macarius is characterized by *a sense of refinement, resignation, and renunciation.* When, for instance, accused of raping the young woman, he said to himself:

> Macarius, you have found yourself a wife. You must work harder now in order to maintain her.[26]

He welcomed accusations as an occasion to remember his limitations. This was his monastic worldview and philosophy.

> The old men said to Abba Macarius: "Father, speak a word to the brothers." He responded: "I have not yet become a monk myself, but I have seen true monks."[27]

> Abba Macarius said: "If slander has become for you the same as praise, poverty as riches, deprivation as abundance, then you will not die."[28]

He was known for "receiving all the brothers in equal simplicity,"[29] for working miracles,[30] but especially for his inclusive love.

> They said of Abba Macarius the Great, that he became, as it were, a god upon this earth; because, just as God protects the world, so Abba Macarius would cover the faults he saw, as though he did not see them, and those he heard, as though he did not hear them.[31]

He too is not demanding in his expectations of others. Although he knew well his own limitations, he was always full of understanding toward the limitations of others. When asked about how one should pray, he responded:

> There is no need at all to make long discourses. It is enough to stretch out one's hands and to say: "Lord, as you will, and as you know, have mercy." And if the conflict grows fiercer, just say: "Lord,

---

26. Macarius 1.
27. Macarius 2.
28. Macarius 20.
29. Macarius 9.
30. Macarius 7, 14, and 15. We shall explore the phenomenon of wonders in the desert later.
31. Macarius 32.

help!" He knows very well what we need, and He shows us His mercy.[32]

And when asked what one should practice, he responded quite simply: do a good deed; say a good word!

> One evil word makes even the good evil. On the other hand, one good word makes even the evil good.[33]

## Abba Moses the Robber

Moses was a released slave. An Ethiopian by birth, he was also a gang-leader and robber in Nitria, infamous for his murder and his muscle. At a mature age, he became a monk, and was the disciple of Isidore the Priest. In his *Lausiac History*,[34] Palladius informs us that Moses once tied up four robbers who entered his own home after he had become a monk. He lifted them all together and brought them to church; all four remained to become monks! Abba Moses was martyred by barbarian invaders around 375. Twenty sayings in all have been preserved under Moses' name.

If there is one desert trait that is classically portrayed in Moses, it is *the virtue of complete renunciation*. What he lived as a robber, he tried to reverse as a monk. His fellow-monks once said to him:

> Abba Moses, you did not keep the laws of society, but it was only so that you might now keep the commandments of heaven.[35]

He spent the rest of his life appreciating and applying the inner work of repentance and resurrection.

> Abba Moses said: "The monk must die to his neighbor and never judge him at all, in any way whatever." When asked what this means, he responded: "If someone does not think in one's heart that one is already dead three days and in the tomb, then that person cannot attain this saying."[36]

---

32. Macarius 19.
33. Macarius 39.
34. See E.C. Butler, *The Lausiac History of Palladius* (Cambridge: Cambridge University Press, 1898-1904), ch. 19; see also the edition edited by R.T. Meyer (Westminster MD: Newman Press, 1965). Palladius traveled through Egypt and met with many of the early hermits; others he heard about during his travels.
35. Moses 5.
36. Moses 14 and 12.

This inner work of tilling the earth of the soul was grueling, almost cruel.

> Abba Zacharias drew his hood off his head, put it under his feet, and trampled on it. Then he said to Abba Moses: "If one does not allow others to treat him in this way, then one cannot become a monk."[37]

Having thus violently (cf. Matt. 11.12) broken the force of his old habits and after many long years softened his earlier hardness, which had become like a second nature to him, Abba Moses could be described by Macarius—that very "god upon this earth"—as "a very sensitive man [literally, a soft nature!]."[38]

## Amma Syncletica

One of the three women that feature in the *Sayings* is Amma Syncletica. Born in 380 in Alexandria, of a wealthy and well-respected pious family, she enjoyed a good education, even being influenced by the more erudite of the Desert Fathers, including Evagrius of Pontus. When her parents died, she sold her belongings and distributed the money to the poor. Together with her sister, who was blind, she lived the life of a hermit, living—like Antony first did—among the tombs just outside of the city. Gradually a number of women gathered around her, and Syncletica served as their spiritual mother, particularly stressing such qualities as *patience and gentleness*. She died around the year 460. Twenty-seven of her sayings are preserved in the alphabetical collection, while a fifth-century account of her life also survives.[39]

Amma Syncletica rejects any sharp distinction between those who live in the desert and those who live in the city. The goal is the same for all, even if the way differs for some. The way of the desert is not the monopoly of the monks. Indeed, in her opinion, there are many people in the world who behave as though they were dwelling in the desert, and vice versa.

37. Zacharias 3.
38. Macarius 22.
39. See *Vita Sanctae Syncleticae* (PG 28: 1488-1557). For Antony, see *Life of Antony*, chapters 8-10.

Amma Syncletica said: "There are many who live in the mountains and behave as if they were in the town; they are wasting their time. It is possible to be a solitary in one's mind while living in a crowd; and it is possible for those who are a solitaries to live in the crowd of their own thoughts."[40]

*Moderation and balance* generally seem to characterize the sayings of this desert *amma*. Syncletica says:

We who have chosen this way of life must obtain perfect temperance.[41]

Everyone has the potential for such balance, she believes; "it is true even among secular people also."[42] Yet, monastics need to move beyond the mere potential of secular people.

Worldly people esteem the culinary art; but you, through fasting and thanks to simple food, should move beyond their abundance of food.[43]

So how are we to distinguish between the divine or royal asceticism and the demonic tyranny? Clearly, it is through the quality of balance.[44]

However, asceticism was not to be regarded as an end in itself. There are times, Syncletica would feel, when the problems in our life are of themselves sufficient ascetic struggle, if endured thankfully. There is no need to overburden the body with further labors of fasting.

Truly, fasting and sleeping on the ground are set before us on account of our sensuality. However, if illness weakens this sensuality, then the reason for these practices is superfluous. For this is the great asceticism: to control oneself in illness and to sing hymns of thanksgiving to God.[45]

She was known for her gift in discerning the spirits. It comes as no surprise, then, to see how Amma Syncletica could also clearly distinguish between the wrong committed and the person committing

40. Syncletica 19.
41. Syncletica 2.
42. *Ibid.*
43. Syncletica 4.
44. Syncletica 15.
45. Syncletica 8.

the wrong, between the crime and the criminal. The sin is to be avoided; the sinner is to be embraced.

> Why hate the person who has harmed you? It is not the person who has done the wrong. Hate the sickness, but do not hate the sick person.[46]

It is a principle upheld also by Abba Zosimas:

> In effect, God has placed us in an order of many members, which have Christ our God as their head, as the Apostle said: "Just as the body is one and has many members, and the head of all is Christ" (1 Cor. 12.12). Therefore, when your brother afflicts you, he is hurting you like a hand or an eye that suffers from some illness. Yet, even when we are in pain, we do not cut off our hand and throw it away; nor do we pull out our eye; indeed, we consider the rejection of each of these as being a very serious matter. Instead, we mark these bodily members with the sign of Christ, which is more precious than anything else, and entreat the saints to pray for them, as well as offering our own fervent prayers to God on their behalf. In addition to this, we apply medication and plaster in order to heal the sore member. Therefore, in the same way that you pray for your eye or your hand in order to heal and no longer hurt, you should also do for your brother.[47]

One of the great tenets of the desert tradition is that all of us "should expect temptations until our last breath."[48] Abba Zosimas always vividly remembered this desert principle:

> He used to say: "Take away the thoughts, and no one can become holy. One who avoids a beneficial temptation is avoiding eternal life."[49]

Amma Syncletica affirms the same conviction:

> Here below, we are not exempt from temptations.[50]

> She also said: "Those who are great athletes must contend against stronger enemies."[51]

---

46. Syncletica 13.
47. *Reflections* VI, c.
48. Antony 4. See also Agathon 9.
49. *Reflections* IV, a.
50. Syncletica 25.
51. Syncletica 14.

*31*

These, then, are some of the key personalities in the fourth-century desert of Egypt. It is now time to turn to turn to the key principles of their teaching.

# FOUR

# *The Desert as Space*

Why did these elders choose the desert in the first place? What was the significance of the desert? What is the power of its suggestion?

"Desert" (*eremos*, ἔρημος) literally means "abandonment"; it is the term from which we derive the word "hermit". The areas of desertedness were where the demons bred. In the Book of Leviticus, the desert is the place that is accursed (Lev.16.21). There is no water in the desert, and in the mind of the Jews that was the ultimate curse. No water also meant no life. The desert signified death: nothing grows in the desert. Your very existence is, therefore, threatened. In the desert you will find no one and no thing. In the desert, you can only face up to yourself and to every aspect of your self, to your temptations, and to your reality. You confront your own heart, and your heart's deepest desires, without any scapegoat, without any hiding place. It is in the desert that Jacob battled; and it is in the desert that you do battle with the unruly forces of your nature within and without. The desert was filled with the presence of the demonic.

> Abba Elias said: "An old man was living in a temple of the desert, and the demons came to him, saying: 'Leave this place; it belongs to us.'"[1]

Yet, the desert was also endowed with sacred significance for Jews and Christians alike. The Israelites had wandered in the desert for forty years. It was there that Moses saw God. It was there that John the Baptist preached the coming of the Messiah. Indeed, it was in the desert that Jesus Himself began His ministry; it was in the wilderness that He was first tempted by the demons (Matt. 4.1-10); and it was in the craggy areas of the Judaean mountains that He

1. Elias 7.

33

periodically withdrew to be alone and to pray (Matt. 14.23). In fact, the early monks believed that a reference in the Letter to the Galatians may also imply a brief sojourn by Paul in the desert of Arabia immediately following his conversion.

> When God, who had set me apart before I was born and called me through His grace, was pleased to reveal His Son to me, so that I might proclaim Him among the Gentiles, I did not confer with any human being, nor did I go up to Jerusalem to those who were already apostles before me, but I went away at once into Arabia, and afterward I returned to Damascus. (Gal. 1.15-17)

So the desert, while accursed, was never seen as an empty region. It was a place that was full of action. It was not an area of scenic views, in the modern sense of a tourist attraction. It was a space that provided an opportunity, and even a calling, for divine vision. In the desert, you were invited to shake off all forms of idolatry, all kinds of earthly limitations, in order to behold—or, rather, to be held before—an image of the heavenly God. There, you were confronted with another reality, with the presence of a boundless God, whose grace was without any limits at all. You could never avoid that perspective of revelation. After all, you cannot hide in the desert; there is no room for lying or deceit there. Your very self is reflected in the dry desert, and you are obliged to face up to this self. Anything else would constitute a dangerous illusion, not a divine icon. Abba Alonius states this quite simply:

> Abba Alonius said: "If one does not say in one's heart, that in the world there is only myself and God, then one will simply not gain peace."[2]

The desert is an attraction beyond oneself; it is an invitation to transfiguration. It was neither a better way, nor an easier way. The desert elders were not out to prove a point; they were there to prove themselves. Antony advises complete renunciation in this effort to hold God before one's eyes at all times:

> Abba Antony also said: "Always have the fear of God before your eyes. Remember Him who gives death and life. Hate the world and all that is in it. Hate all peace that comes from the flesh. Renounce this life, so that you may be alive to God. Remember what you have

2. Alonius 1.

promised God, for it will be required of you on the Day of Judgment. Suffer hunger; suffer thirst; suffer nakedness; be watchful and sorrowful; weep and groan in your heart; test yourselves, to see if you are worthy of God; despise the flesh, so that you may preserve your souls."[3]

Nothing should be held back in this surrender. It is all or nothing. The abandonment to God is absolute. As a result, the rewards are either fruitful or else frightening.

> A brother renounced the world and gave his goods to the poor. However, he kept back just a little for his personal expenses and needs. He went to see Abba Antony. When he told him of this, the old man said to him: "If you want to be a monk, go into the village, buy some meat, cover your naked body with this meat, and then come here like that." The brother did so. And the dogs and birds tore at his flesh. When he came back, the old man asked him whether he had followed his advice. The brother simply showed Antony his wounded body. Saint Antony said: "Those who renounce the world but choose to keep back even a little for themselves are torn in this way by the demons."[4]

The desert is a place of spiritual revolution, not of personal retreat. It is a place of inner protest, not outward peace. It is a place of deep encounter, not of superficial escape. It is a place of repentance, not recuperation. Living in the desert does not mean living without people; it means living for God. Antony and the other desert dwellers never forgot this. They never sought to cut off their connections to other people instantly. They sought rather to refine these relationships increasingly.

Of course, the desert was, on a deeper level, always more than simply a place. It was a way. And it was not the desert that made the Desert Fathers and Mothers, any more than it was the lion that made the martyrs.[5] The *Sayings* contain many stories that reveal the desert as a spiritual way that was present everywhere, including the large and busy cities.

> It was revealed to Abba Antony in his desert that there was someone who was his equal in the city. He was a doctor by profes-

3. Antony 33.
4. Antony 20.
5. Cf. *The Wisdom of the Desert Fathers*, ed. B Ward (Oxford: SLG Press, 1975), p. vii (Foreword by Anthony Bloom).

sion. Whatever he had beyond his needs, he would give to the poor; and every day he sang hymns with the angels.[6]

It is the clear understanding of these elders that one does not have to move to the geographical location of the wilderness in order to find God. Yet, if you do not have to *go to the desert*, you do have to *go through the desert*. The Desert Fathers and Mothers always *speak from* their experience of the desert, even if they do not actually come out of that desert. The desert is a necessary stage on the spiritual journey. To avoid it would be harmful. To dress it up or conceal it may be tempting; but it also proves destructive in the spiritual path.

Ironically, you do not have to find the desert in your life; it normally catches up with you. Everyone does go through the desert, in one shape or another. It may be in the form of some suffering, or emptiness, or breakdown, or breakup, or divorce, or any kind of trauma that occurs in our life. Dressing this desert up through our addictions or attachments—to material goods, or money, or food, or drink, or success, or obsessions, or anything else we may care to turn toward or may find available to depend upon—will delay the utter loneliness and the inner fearfulness of the desert experience. If we go through this experience involuntarily, then it can be both overwhelming and crushing. If, however, we accept to undergo this experience voluntarily, then it can prove both constructive and liberating.

The physical setting of the desert is a symbol, a powerful reminder of a spiritual space that is within us all. In the United States, the grand desert of Arizona can assist us in recalling that inner space where we yearn for God. In Australia, the frightening outback can also guide us in our search for that heavenly "dreamtime." In Egypt, the sandy dunes of the desert resembled the unending search of these *abbas* and *ammas* for "abundant life" (John 10.10) and "a living spring of water" (John 4.14).

6. Antony 24. See also K. Ware, "The Monk and the Married Christian," *Eastern Churches Review* 6 (1974): 72-83.

# The Struggle against Demons

Abba Alonius says that, in the presence of God, you face up to your self in the desert. In the desert, you discover your true self, without any masks or myths. There you are forced to come to terms with your self. Ultimately, you are called to face up to and fight against your demons, without blaming either someone else or your past.

> Abba Antony said to Abba Poemen: "This is the great work of a person: always to take the blame for one's own sins before God and to expect temptation to one's last breath."[1]

Assuming the blame for your own sins is by no means identical to avoiding confrontation with others. It means refusing to be victimized. It implies freedom and control over one's life. If you are not in control of what you do, then someone else is in control of your life and you are dis-empowered from any action at all. The first step in personal change can only come from within. Assuming responsibility for your life, and doing something about it, is the beginning of a truly creative and meaningful life. In any case, these desert elders knew very well that, even if we have not directly committed a particular wrong, nevertheless our actions—and especially our attitudes—may in fact contribute to the general conditions that allow particular wrongs to occur. We all influence one another's spiritual choices. We are all involved in one another's spiritual growth.

Therefore, each experience of temptation and each circumstance of pain comprise a treasure and a blessing through which we become, together, more integrated. It is collectively that we are both complemented and completed. In fact, the Greek word for "salva-

---

1. Antony 4. Abba Zosimas further believes that when one blames others, one is in fact substituting the role of the demons within oneself! See *Reflections* VII, c.

tion" (*soteria*, σωτηρία) indicates precisely a sense of wholeness and integrity. There are, then, no other options; there is no other way but to face the temptations head-on. It almost appears that the desert elders are grateful for them.

> Abba Evagrius said: "Take away temptations and no one will be saved."[2]

> Abba Poemen said: "Even if a person were to create a new heaven and earth, one could not live free of care."[3]

> Abba Antony said: "Whoever has not experienced temptation cannot enter into the kingdom of heaven." He even added: "Without temptations no one can be saved."[4]

The teaching is fairly clear: *if my devils leave me, then my angels will too.* The Desert Fathers and Mothers are not overwhelmed by temptation. They regard it as a way—perhaps the only sure way—of encountering God. There can be no gain without pain. Amma Theodora used pictorial language:

> Amma Theodora said: "Let us strive to enter by the narrow gate. Just as the trees cannot bear fruit if they have not stood before the winter's storms, so it is with us. This present age is a storm; and it is only through many trials and temptations that we can obtain an inheritance in the kingdom of heaven."[5]

In the stories about the temptations faced by Jesus Christ in the wilderness, it was only after struggling against the demons three times—which could be interpreted as thirty-three times, which could in turn be interpreted as an ongoing struggle—that we are told of "the angels coming and ministering unto Him" (Matt. 4.11). Our spiritual struggle enables us first to see, then to understand, and finally to embrace our limitations and failures. The Desert Fathers and Mothers confess—and then, ultimately, profess—a spirituality of imperfection. They do not conceal—nor do they presume to know any "magical" ways around—these imperfections.

We are to recognize our deeper emotions, and especially our motivations, if we are to grow in the way of life and of love. We are

2. Evagrius 5.
3. Poemen 48.
4. Antony 5.
5. Theodora 2.

to become conscious of our inner desires and personal weaknesses, to confront and accept them in uncompromising simplicity and radical sincerity, without any rationalization or complication. This is what the Desert Fathers and Mothers struggled to do. There are *no ways around* this struggle; there are *only ways through* the struggle. There is only hard labor and much patience. Toil (*kopos*, κόπος) is a desert virtue, the starting-point and basis for every other virtue.

> One of the Fathers asked Abba John the Dwarf: "What is a monk?" He replied: "A monk is toil. The monk toils in everything. That is what a monk is."[6]

6. John the Dwarf 37.

# SIX

## *The Patience of the Cell*

In the struggle of patience, the Desert Fathers and Mothers recommend that we remain in what they call the "cell". The Greek term for "patience" (*hupomone*, ὑπομονή) literally implies just sitting there, simply staying put! Abba Macarius offers a stark directive in a stark desert:

Stay in your cell.[1]

The cell is the simple hut or room, where the monastic lives alone. In the cell, you *simply stay with yourself*; you sit with your emotions; and you shut the door to any intrusion.

It was said of Abba Sisoes that when he was sitting in the cell, he would always close the door.[2]

The cell is the starting-point; in fact, it is also the ending-point.

A brother came to Scetis to visit Abba Moses and asked him for a word. The old man said to him: "Go, sit in your cell, and your cell will teach you everything."[3]

If we consider prematurely the various virtues taught by the desert, then we reduce its powerful symbolism to some code of good conduct. Abba Gelasius would formulate it in this way:

If you are not able to perform the works of the desert, then live patiently in your cell . . . without wandering here and there.[4]

A brother asked Abba Sisoes: "Why did you leave Scetis, where you lived with Abba Or and come to live here?" The old man said: "At the time when Scetis became crowded, I heard that Antony was

1. Macarius 41.
2. Sisoes 24.
3. Moses 6.
4. Gelasius 6.

dead and I got up and came here to the mountain. Finding the place peaceful, I have settled here for a little while." The brother asked him: "How long have you been here?" The old man replied: "Seventy-two years."[5]

The temptation in the spiritual life is to move away from the temptation, to avoid the pain.

> Blessed Syncletica said: "If you find yourself in a monastery, do not go to another place. For that will harm you a great deal. Just as the bird that abandons the eggs she was sitting on prevents them from hatching, so the monk or the nun grow cold and their faith dies, when they go from one place to another."[6]

Abba Antony puts it more bluntly:

> Just as fish die if they stay too long out of water, so the monks who loiter outside their cell or pass their time with worldly people lose the intensity of inner peace. So like fish going toward the sea, we must hurry to reach our cell, for fear that if we delay outside we shall lose our interior watchfulness.[7]

The cell symbolizes the work of the soul. Like the desert, it too is not merely a place; it is a profound way of the spirit.

> One day Abba Daniel and Abba Ammoe went on a journey together. Abba Ammoe said: "When shall we, too, settle in a cell, Father?" Abba Daniel replied: "Who shall separate us henceforth from God? God is in the cell; but, on the other hand, God is outside the cell too."[8]

> Abba Ammonas said: "Go, sit in your cell, and engrave it on your heart."[9]

The stability that is here called for is not physical but spiritual. The whole mystery of the desert is encapsulated in this one concept of the cell.

> Abba Isaiah questioned Abba Macarius, saying: "Give me a word, Abba." The old man said to him: "Flee from the world." Abba

5. Sisoes 28.
6. Syncletica 6.
7. Antony 10. See also Theodore of Pherme 14.
8. Daniel 5.
9. Poemen 2.

> Isaiah asked: "What does it mean to flee from the world?" The old man replied: "It means to sit in your cell and weep for your sins."[10]

The reality of the cell should spill over into the reality of our life. The boundaries of our cell are gradually expanded to include every moment in our life and every detail in our world.

> Abba Serinus said: "There is no great virtue in keeping to your discipline in your cell. But there is, if you also keep it when you come out of your cell."[11]

The cell becomes the place where we encounter God, the place where God is.

> A certain old man asked God to allow him to meet all the Fathers; and he saw them all except Abba Antony. So he asked his guide: "Where is Abba Antony?" He was told by way of reply: "In the place where God is, there Antony would also be."[12]

If the cell indicates the space and the place where we are able to encounter God, then patience intimates the framework or the time within which such an encounter will occur.

> Abba Arsenius said to someone who was tempted by the demons: "Go, eat, drink, do no work; only do not leave your cell." For he knew that patience in the cell keeps a monk in the right way.[13]

"Evil thoughts and demons disappear through patience," claimed Abba Poemen. Patience is something you pray for fervently. Once gained, however, it can even heal the sick![14]

10. Macarius 27.
11. Serinus 1.
12. Antony 28.
13. Arsenius 11.
14. Poemen 21. See also Poemen 102; John the Dwarf 13; and Isidore 1.

# Silence and Tears

What one comes to practice in patience is the virtue of silence (*hesychia*, ἡσυχία). We come to self-knowledge through stillness and silence, through attentiveness and watchfulness (*nepsis*, νῆψις). When words are abandoned, a new awareness arrives. Silence awakens us from dullness of awareness, from dimness of vision.

> Abba Bessarion, at the point of his death, said: "The monk ought to be as the cherubim and the seraphim: all eye!"[1]

> Abba Poemen said: "Be watchful inwardly; and be watchful outwardly."[2]

Silence is the first duty of life, the first requirement for survival in the desert.

> Having withdrawn to the desert, Abba Arsenius . . . heard a voice saying to him: "Arsenius, flee; be silent; pray always. These are the source of sinlessness."[3]

Silence is also the first duty of love (*agape*, ἀγάπη), the first requirement for survival within community.

> Abba Poemen said: "Someone may seem to be silent, but if in the heart one is condemning others, then one is babbling ceaselessly. And there may be another who talks from morning till evening, and yet in the heart that person is truly silent. That person says nothing that is not profitable."[4]

Silence is *a way of waiting, a way of watching, and a way of listening* to what is going on within and around us. It is a way of interiority, of stopping and then of exploring the cellars of the heart and the

---

1. Bessarion 11.
2. Poemen 137.
3. Arsenius 2.
4. Poemen 27.

center of life. It is a way of entering within, so that we do not ultimately go without. Silence is never merely a cessation of words; that would be too restrictive and too negative a definition of silence. Rather, it is the pause that holds together—indeed, it makes sense of—all the words, both spoken and unspoken. Silence is the glue that connects our attitudes and our actions. Silence is fullness, not emptiness; it is not an absence, but the awareness of a presence. The entire flight to the desert may be summarized in this priority and practice of silence.

> Abba Macarius the Great said to the brothers at Scetis: "Flee, my brothers." One of the old men asked him: "Where else could we flee beyond this desert?" Macarius placed his finger on his lips and said: "Flee that!" And he went into his cell, shut the door, and sat down.[5]

> A brother came to see Abba Poemen in the second week of Lent, and told him about his thoughts. He obtained peace, and said to him: "I nearly did not come here today." The old man asked him why. The brother said: "I said to myself: 'Perhaps he will not let me in because it is Lent.'" Abba Poemen said to him: "We have been taught not to close the wooden door, but to close the door of our tongues."[6]

The reality is, of course, that we tend to be impatient; we tend to wander; we tend to interfere with the process. And so we are tempted to speak; we break the deafening silence. Words are ways of affirming our existence, of justifying our actions. We speak in order to excuse ourselves, within ourselves and before others; whereas silence is a way of dying—within ourselves and in the presence of others. It is a way of surrendering life, always in the context and in the hope of new life and resurrection.

> Abba Alonius said: "If I had not destroyed myself completely, I would not have been able to rebuild and reshape myself again."[7]

Abba Alonius' words may sound very harsh. Yet, it may be that by surrendering life we can find ourselves again. In struggling against what we are not, we are in fact seeking to discover what we

5. Macarius 16.
6. Poemen 58.
7. Alonius 2.

truly are. The reality is that we tend to forget who and what we truly are. When we refuse the challenge of silence, then we cannot know ourselves. It is not that we may be tempted to think that we are more than we actually are; it is, unfortunately, then that we tolerate being *less than we truly are called to be.* Pride is not the ultimate sin; forgetfulness of who we are is the ultimate tragedy. This is why the wisdom of the desert emphasized remembrance of death; it was the other side of the same coin, which may be called remembrance of God.

> When the death of Arsenius drew near, the brothers saw him weeping and asked: "Truly, Father, are you afraid?" "Indeed," he answered them, "the fear which is mine at this hour has been with me ever since I became a monk."[8]

Yet, silence does not come easily. If silence is the language of God, the language they speak in Heaven, then is it any wonder that we make so many mistakes in interpreting this language? It can never be an easy task to be willing to place ourselves at the threshold of the heavenly kingdom, or like Abba Arsenius to stand at the verge of death.

> It was said of Abba Agathon that for three years he lived with a stone in his mouth, until he had learned to keep silence.[9]

The Desert Fathers and Mothers embraced their mortality; they were comfortable with death. They recognized death as another form of community, as another profound way of connection to themselves, to their neighbor and to God as the Lord of life and death. So often, we endeavor to cheat death; we instinctively try to avoid or escape it. We do not want to face change, or pain, or passion, or death. In desert terminology, that would be the temptation to move outside the cell. The image of "living death" is perhaps far more terrifying to us than death itself. And so, we search for ways to step away from death—financially, technologically, medically, emotionally. Words are a part of our rational selves; to abandon words is to give way to our spiritual selves. Nevertheless, the Desert Fathers and Mothers advise us to stay silent and to stay put! They counsel us to shut the door and to sit in the cell! We are simply to wait, even

8. Arsenius 41.
9. Agathon 15. See also Sisoes 30: "Even to the point of death, monks should control themselves so as not to speak."

as—indeed, *especially* when—we experience moments of panic, of powerlessness, of helplessness, of terror, of death. That is what they did. After all, where do you go beyond the desert? Where else do you go when you have climbed a thirty-foot pole, as the stylites of Syria did?[10] Where can you go when, like Antony, you have moved from the outer desert to the inner desert of Egypt? You just sit; you just stay; you just wait. Then, when you arrive at the end of your individual resources, an infinite and eternal source can open up. Not that divine grace is absent beforehand; it is simply unnoticed, while we yet depend on ourselves.

So, you just wait there. You wait and you hope. More particularly, *you wait and you weep.* Tears (*dakrya*, δάκρυα) and weeping (*penthos*, πένθoς) indicate a significant frontier in the way of the desert. They bespeak a promise. In fact, they are the only way into the heart.

> Abba Poemen said: "One who wishes to purify one's faults purifies them with tears; one who wishes to acquire the virtues acquires them with tears. Weeping is the way that the Scriptures and the Fathers give us, when they say: 'Weep!' Truly, there is no other way than this."[11]

Arsenius is said to have carved a hole in his chest from continual weeping!

> It was said of Abba Arsenius that he had a hollow in his chest channeled out by the tears, which fell from his eyes all through his life while he sat doing his manual work. When Abba Poemen learned that he was dead, he said weeping: "Truly you are blessed, Abba Arsenius, for you wept for yourself in this world. One who does not weep here below will weep eternally hereafter. So it is impossible not to weep, either voluntarily or when compelled through suffering."[12]

The desert elders appreciate human sin and failure as the ultimate opportunity for divine grace and strength, which can only be "perfected in weakness" (2 Cor. 12.9). This is precisely the framework within which they understand the role of tears. Early on, we seem to lose that innate ability to grieve; and so we must learn, grad-

---

10. See *The Lives of Symeon Stylites*, ed. R. Doran (Kalamazoo MI: Cistercian Publications, 1992).
11. Poemen 119.
12. Arsenius 41.

ually and painfully, to acquire it again. Tears are unfortunately often perceived as a negative aspect of the spiritual life. Few comprehend that tears of brokenness, as symbols of imperfection, are in fact the *sole* way of spiritual progress.

Abba Poemen also said: "Truly, there is no other way than this!"[13]

These desert dwellers do not like to speak about metaphysical matters or about spiritual perfection. They simply record the details of a long journey, the painful steps along the way, and the gradual stages towards this sublime goal of perfection. They recognize that this alone is within our grasp and realism. One silent tear will advance us more in the spiritual way than any number of "louder" ascetic feats or more "visible" virtuous achievements.

The silence of tears reflects our surrender to God and to new patterns of learning and living. Through weeping, we learn by suffering and undergoing, not just by speculating and understanding. The connection between tears and silence is important in this context. Tears are another way, a tangible way of addressing our pain and our panic. They are another, a passionate way of knowing our passions. They are the articulation of our grief, the wording of our desire. The greater our love, the greater the corresponding sense of grief. It is the depth of our love that determines the intensity of our weeping. Through tears, we give up our infantile images of God and give in to the living image of God. We confess our personal powerlessness and profess divine powerfulness. Tears confirm our readiness to allow our life to fall apart in the dark night of the soul, and our willingness to assume new life in the resurrection of the dead. It is the grace to accept and appreciate that our limited perspective of life should be forgone in the light of an unlimited perspective of full life.

Abba Alonius said: "If I had not destroyed myself completely, I would not have been able to rebuild and reshape myself again."

He also said: "If only a person truly desired for a single day, from morning till night, that person would be able to come to the measure of God."[14]

13. Poemen 119.
14. Alonius 2 and 3.

When we admit our hopelessness and desperation, when we recognize that we have "hit rock bottom" in ourselves as well as in our relationships with people and with God, we also discover the compassion of a God who voluntarily assumed the vulnerability of crucifixion. One would not seek divine healing unless one had to in order to survive, unless one admitted there was no other way out of the impasse.

Our hearts are the dwelling-places of God. Yet, all of them are made of fragile glass. Tears signify the fragility of the heart. They expose the brokenness and vulnerability of the soul. They allow for clearer vision into the world of the heart. Tears open up the festering wound; and, ironically—the desert elders would say: miraculously—God enters through this very wound. God enters the open wound—the shattered window—of our heart and brings healing to the soul and the world, not in order merely to comfort, but rather to identify completely with us in an act of infinite compassion. The God that these desert elders worship understands; that God has undergone the vulnerability of assuming child-likeness and death on a cross. This vulnerability is the only way toward holiness. The more profound our personal misery, the more abundant God's eternal mercy. The deeper the abyss of our human corruption, the greater the grace of heavenly compassion. The more involved our exposure to the way of the cross, the more intense our experience of the light of resurrection.

As with so much else in *The Sayings of the Desert Fathers*, their stories about the gift of tears are a testimony, not a teaching. Yet the desert elders reveal extraordinarily subtle insights into the mysterious land of tears, into the complexity of tears, their status and significance in spiritual life. Their experience of tears resembles an expression of depth, revealing the fragility of life and unveiling a spirituality of imperfection. Desert spirituality underlines imperfection as the only way toward perfection. There is, quite simply, nothing beyond watching, waiting in, and weeping for our imperfections. For the Desert Fathers and Mothers, there is no stage beyond this knowledge of imperfection. Perfection is for God, not for us; imperfection is ours to know and embrace, not to forego or forget. In the desert, the Gospel injunction to "be perfect, as your heavenly Father is perfect" (Matt. 5.48) becomes a vision of realism. It does not remain some vague dream or romanticism, but is perceived through the lenses of reality. For these elders, life is a continual balance of tensions, a perpetual standing beneath the cross, an unceasing weeping. And the source, the object of these tears is the light of the resurrection that shines beyond the cross, transforming sorrow into joy. This was the conviction that was passed down through generations in the desert of Egypt.

> Abba Joseph related that Abba Isaac said: "I was sitting with Abba Poemen one day, and I saw him in ecstasy. And, as I was on terms of great freedom of speech with him, I prostrated myself before him and begged him saying: 'Tell me where you were.' He was forced to answer and said: 'My thought was with Saint Mary, the Mother of God, as she wept by the cross of the Savior. I wish I could always weep like that.'"[15]

Tears signify an opening of new life, a softening of the soul, a clarity of the mind. They bring us to rebirth and the world to healing. They signify a true homecoming. Through tears we are able to enter the treasury of the heart. And then, when we allow our heart to be broken, when we allow our life, as we know it, to fall apart, we are free to be reborn and—quite simply—to be more and more. The ultimate form of renunciation in the desert is letting go of life. As we shall see below, what is far more important than learning to live is in fact learning to die.

15. Poemen 144.

# The Treasury of the Heart

Abba Pambo said: "If you have a heart, you can be saved."[1]

When we wait and weep, what do we know? Once we enter the heart (*kardia*, καρδία), what do we then discover? This is perhaps the essence of the desert message. What we discover is that we are not in control of ourselves, that we are wounded. We discover our passions (*pathe*, πάθη), which are sometimes naïvely identified with sins or vices, but which are much more than this. *Passions are our inner wounds*, those deep marks in the space of our heart that require healing. In the mind of the desert elders, this means that they need to be attended to and tended. If we are going to be a healing presence in the world, then we need to comprehend our passions. In fact, we need, as we shall see below, even to embrace these passions. In order to be truly alive, we require the capacity to be wounded, to be vulnerable. It is only out of our ongoing woundedness and continual vulnerability that we can learn also to heal. Passions express our ability to be passionate; they exemplify our ability to be loved as well as our capacity to love. In brief, the desert elders are icons of this vulnerability.

There are, of course, many different kinds of passions. There are passions of nature and passions of nurture. Nevertheless, our passions indicate not so much that we are doing something wrong, but that we are not in control. The word "passion" is derived from the Greek term *pathos*, which indicates that we are—as the English word itself also implies—passive rather than active. It may be up to us, as we shall see, to direct these passions toward life or toward our destruction; toward hope or else toward despair; toward either a disposition of grief or else of gratitude. However, in the state of pas-

1. Pambo 10.

sion, more is being done to us than we are actually doing to others or to ourselves. Abba Zosimas expressed it in the following manner:

> It was well said once by a wise person, that the soul has as many masters as it has passions. And again, the Apostle says: "People are slaves to whatever masters them" (2 Pet. 2.19).[2]

Another way of considering passions is to view them as habits. There may be habits of seeing, of hearing, of feeling, of thinking, of acting. These habits are lasting, often reflecting short-cuts that we have grown accustomed to in responding to our habitat.

> Abba Poemen said that Abba Ammonas said: "A person may remain in the cell for a hundred years without learning how to live in the cell."[3]

These are also habits, which have hardened over time, becoming like a second nature to us. Hence the grueling battle to break them, to redirect them. We may recall here the terrifying story from the *Life of Antony*:

> Antony entered one of the tombs, shut the door behind him, and remained there alone. And the enemy . . . came one night with a multitude of demons, cutting him and beating him, so that Antony lay on the ground speechless from the extreme pain inflicted by the demons. Indeed, he affirmed that the torture had been so excessive that no blows caused by a human being could ever have brought such suffering . . . The next day, when Antony's friend opened the door of the tomb, he saw Antony lying there on the ground as if he was dead. He lifted him up and carried him to the church in the village, and laid him down on the ground. Many of his relatives and the villagers gathered around Antony, like people gather around a corpse. Then, about midnight, Antony came to himself and awoke . . . though he could not stand up on account of the demonic blows.[4]

Therefore, these habits must be addressed as early as possible.

> Abba Joseph asked Abba Sisoes: "For how long must a person cut away the passions?" The old man replied: "Do you want to know how long?" Abba Joseph answered: "Yes." Then the old man said to him: "So long as a passion attacks you, cut it away at once."[5]

2. *Reflections* V, ii, c.
3. Poemen 96.
4. Chapters 8-9.
5. Sisoes 22.

This is because such passions or habits distort the reality of who we are and of what our world is. They blind us and lead us to compulsive acts. And so we cannot respond appropriately. We cannot be fully alive; and this sense of "having life" is also implied in the original Latin term *habito*.

Abba Zosimas' *Reflections* speak of addressing and redirecting our habits positively:

> When someone learns this art well and practices it, gradually, by exercising it, it becomes like a second nature to the doctor or the sophist. Then such people cannot explain or express how this habit occurred gradually . . . and how imperceptibly it has seized their soul, simply by practicing the art. The same also happens in the case of humility. For, from the keeping of the commandments, a certain habitual humility occurs, which cannot be explained in words.[6]

I have already mentioned that we are required to address our passions. In the language of the desert, this is called *knowing* the passions. The term knowing has very intimate, even sexual connotations in biblical and ascetic literature. Knowing means loving; it implies embracing. It is a way of being aware of oneself within one's environment. In the ascetic tradition, there are in fact two ways of understanding and responding to the passions. There is, on the one hand, the view of passions as something negative. This derives from the more Stoic understanding of sins or vices, whereby these are perceived to be a disorder, a disease or an infection. According to this view, passions are intrinsically evil; they are a pathological condition. Moreover, their source is the devil.

If this is one's understanding of passions, then they should be eradicated; our struggle is for them to be eliminated. There can be no discussion or flirtation with them; they must quite simply be suppressed and destroyed. Certainly, there is ample information in the *Sayings* to support this conception about the passions and our corresponding behavior toward them.

> Abba Poemen said: "When David was fighting with the lion, he seized it by the throat and killed it immediately. If we take ourselves by the throat and by the belly, with the help of God, we shall overcome the invisible lion."[7]

6. *Reflections*, "From the Teachings of Abba Dorotheus."
7. Poemen 178.

> Abba Pityrion, the disciple of Abba Antony said: "If anyone wants to drive out the demons, that person must first subdue the passions. For, then, the demon of the passion that is mastered will also be banished. For example, the devil accompanies anger; so if you control your anger, the devil of anger will be banished. And so it is with each of the passions."[8]

However, this is not the only view of passions among the Desert Fathers and Mothers. There is, on the other hand, the view of passions as something positive. This conveys the more Aristotelian understanding of sins or vices, whereby passions are perceived as neutral forces, even natural impulses. According to this view, passions are intrinsically objective; they are neither good nor evil, neither right nor wrong. Moreover, their source is actually God. It depends on us whether these passions are to be put to good use or not. It is up to us whether they are to be directed toward their proper end and purpose. Passions are right or wrong only inasmuch as they affect us, or rather to the degree that we allow them to affect us. If this is one's prevailing concept of passions, then these should be educated, not eliminated; the aim is to illumine them, not eliminate them; they are not to be destroyed but mastered and even transfigured.

> Abba Joseph of Panephysis said: "Truly, if the passions enter you and you fight them, you will become stronger. I have spoken to you about myself. But there are others who cannot profit in this way if the passions approach them, and so they must cut them off immediately."[9]

Elsewhere, Joseph is even clearer about mastering, not annihilating the passions:

> Some of the brothers happened one day to meet at Abba Joseph's cell. While they were sitting there, questioning him, he became cheerful and, filled with happiness, he said to them: "I am a king today; for I reign over the passions."[10]

So, in the desert, we discover a whole range of ways in which the passions are addressed and in which we are called to address the passions. Abba Dorotheus would say:

8. Pityrion 1.
9. Joseph of Panephysis 3.
10. Joseph of Panephysis 10.

The body kills me; I kill it![11]

Others would prefer to say that we do not kill the body, but instead that we kill the passions, or cut them away at once:

> Abba Isaac came to see Abba Poemen and found him washing his feet. As he enjoyed freedom of speech with the old man, he asked: "How is it that others practice austerity and treat their bodies harshly?" Abba Poemen replied: "We have not been taught to kill our bodies, but to kill our passions."[12]

Still others would say that we control the passions, but do not kill them at all. Finally, there is the genuinely refreshing and quite remarkable advice offered by Abba Isaiah of Scetis in his remarkable *Ascetic Discourses*.[13] In his second ascetic discourse, Abba Isaiah claims that all of the passions—and he enumerates some of them; they include anger, jealousy, even lust—are given to us by God with a particular and sacred purpose. Unfortunately, writes Isaiah, we have misdirected and misused them, so that they have now come to be regarded as evil. However, the original purpose of anger is for it to be used against injustice in the world; the proper reason for envy is so that we may seek to emulate the virtues of the saints; and the natural goal of our desire is to thirst for God. However, we have bent these natural forces out of shape; and so now we are angry at our neighbor over petty reasons; we are jealous about material things; and we lust after earthly things.

Wrongful passions are a diversion from true passion; by doing evil and hurting others, we are in fact divested of authentic passion. Abba Isaiah also features in *The Sayings of the Desert Fathers*, and indeed Isaiah had experienced life in the desert of Scetis before moving to Palestine in the fifth century. He knew well the inner meaning of the struggle to know the passions. The same line of thought is found in the *Reflections* of Abba Zosimas:

> It is like I always say: Inasmuch as He is good, God has given us to profit from everything. However, we become attached and misuse

---

11. See Palladius, *The Lausiac History*, ch. 2.

12. Poemen 184.

13. See the translation of and introduction to his teaching in J. Chryssavgis and P.R. Penkett, *Abba Isaiah of Scetis: Ascetic Discourses* (Kalamazoo MI: Cistercian Publications, 2002).

God's gifts; and so we turn these very same good gifts to destruction through our evil choice, and are therefore harmed.[14]

This is a radically different way of addressing the passions, because it links passions with the powerful force of desire and love. In modern day parlance, we even speak about our desires as being our passions. These are the things that we are passion-ate about in our life.

> A brother asked Abba Sisoes: "What shall I do about the passions?" The old man said: "Each person is tempted when lured and enticed by personal desire."[15]

Passions were ultimately matters of wanting and willing, of desire and love. In the desert, love and charity were what mattered the most. Passions, therefore, were not to be crushed; they were to be conquered by greater and nobler passions. And when the desert elders speak of *apatheia* or dispassion, they are not in any way promoting any teaching about passion-lessness; still less are they preaching any sense of apathy. Indeed, they would want us to be weaned from any kind of indifference (which they would certainly regard as a vice!) and invite us to become free in order to love genuinely and intensely. We are to address the passions in order to become dis-passionate. Yet, dispassion is not the suppression of passions; it is the submission of all passions to the source and end of all desire, namely "the kingdom of heaven and its righteousness" (Matt. 6.33). It is only then that we may truly know what it is to be com-passionate. Charity and dispassion are distinguishable only by name, resembling two sides of one and the same coin. Abba Evagrius was one of the few who could articulate this in the form of precise theological definitions:

> Abba Evagrius said that one of the Fathers used to say: "Love [or *agape*] is . . . what leads a monk rapidly to the threshold of dispassion [or *apatheia*]."[16]

When passions are distorted, then our soul is divided and we are no longer integrated, whole. The understanding in the desert was that a single vivid experience of authentic, passionate desire for

14. *Reflections* X, d.
15. Sisoes 44.
16. Evagrius 6.

God was sufficient to advance one much more in the ascetic life than any extreme feat of fasting or vigil. In fact, such purified passion, or pure passion, could never be checked or quenched. It could only be filled or fulfilled. True passion and desire does not seek to be stopped or satisfied. It can only grow endlessly.

> Abba Zosimas said: "Our free will is not passionate. If it were passionate, then by the grace of God everything would appear simple for our free will. As I have frequently told you, a small inclination of our desire is able to attract God for our assistance."[17]

The Desert Fathers and Mothers recognized that it takes a long time to become a human being. It takes an infinitely patient waiting to put together all the variegated parts of the human heart. Moreover, in the unnoticeable changes toward ever-growing perfection, it is the things that we love that reveal to us who we are. It is the things to which we are most attached that show us where our priorities lie. It is our very imperfections—what they like to call passions, and what we invariably call our wounds—that lead us to the way of perfection.

Therefore, if we want to honestly discern the passions of our heart, we should consider what we actually like to do and even need to do, or what most characterizes our way of handling life. Some of these passions might include: the desire to gossip or be judgmental; the desire to control or manipulate; the desire for perfectionism; the need for constant approval; the distrust of others or mistrust of ourselves; the fear of stillness or of silence; the tendency toward irritation or agitation; an attitude of impurity or darkness; a lack of self-control; and cravings or addictions of many kinds. In brief, that which makes us feel "high," where we do not have to face reality; that is where our passions often lurk. These are the passions we may need to admit and address.

Then, knowing our passions becomes not a crushing but a healing experience. Then, we no longer excuse bad behavior, but accept our self without delusions. Then, fresh possibilities are discovered in our life and in our world. We perceive new dimensions of reality; we see the same things as before, but now with new eyes. This is why the desert elders, both fathers and mothers alike, prayed

17. *Reflections* VII, d.

not be to be rid of passions, but to be strengthened in their struggle to know them. For passions reveal that we are innately equipped, and by our very nature endowed, with qualities through which we may be healed and renewed in order to move on.

> Abba Poemen said of Abba John the Dwarf that he prayed to God to take his passions away from him so that he might become free from care. He went and told an old man about this: "I find myself in peace, without an enemy," he said. The old man said to him: "Go, beseech God to stir up warfare so that you may regain the affliction and humility that you used to have. For, it is by warfare that the soul makes progress." So he besought God, and when the warfare came, he no longer prayed that it might be taken away, but he said: "Lord, give me strength for the fight."[18]

> It was related of Amma Sarah that for thirteen years she waged warfare against the demon of fornication. She never prayed that the warfare should cease, but only said: "God, give me strength."[19]

In fact, so much part and parcel of their spiritual practice and teaching was this precedence given to acknowledging and knowing the passions, that the more advanced among the desert elders refused to speak about anything else. One of my favorite stories in this regard comes from the collection attributed to Abba Poemen:

> A brother from Abba Poemen's neighborhood left to go to another land one day. There he met a hermit. The latter was very charitable and many visitors came to see him. The brother told him about Abba Poemen. When he heard about his virtue, the hermit wanted to meet Poemen. Some time afterward, when the brother had returned to Egypt, the hermit also went there to see the brother who had formerly paid him a visit. For, he had told him where he lived. When he saw him, the brother was surprised and very pleased. The hermit said to him: "Please, will you be so kind as to take me to Abba Poemen?" So the brother brought him to the old man and presented him, saying: "This is a great man, full of charity, and he is held in high esteem in his own region. I had spoken to him about you, and he has come here because he wants to meet you." So Abba Poemen received the hermit with joy. They greeted one another and sat down. The visitor began to speak of the Scriptures, of spiritual and of heavenly matters. But Abba Poemen turned his face away and answered nothing. Seeing that

18. John the Dwarf 13.
19. Sarah 1.

Poemen did not respond at all, the hermit went away deeply grieved and told the brother who had brought him: "I have made this long journey in vain. For I have come to visit the old man, and he does not even wish to speak to me." Then the brother went inside to Abba Poemen and said to him: "Abba, this great man, who has such a fine reputation in his own land, has come here for you. Why do you not speak to him?" The old man said: "He is indeed great and speaks of heavenly things; and I am lowly and speak of earthly things. If he had spoken to me about the passions of the soul, I would have replied. However, he speaks to me about spiritual things, and I know nothing about these." Then the brother came out and told the visitor: "The old man does not readily speak of the Scriptures, but if anyone consults him about the passions of the soul, he responds." Filled with compunction, the visiting hermit returned to the old man and said to him: "What should I do, Abba, for the passions of the soul control me?" The old man turned toward him and replied joyfully: "This time, you come as you should. Now open your mouth concerning these matters, and I shall fill it with good things." Greatly edified, the hermit said to him: "Truly, this is the right way!" He returned to his own region giving thanks to God that he had been counted worthy to meet so great a saint.[20]

This was the way of the desert. And in this way, the emphasis was—at least for the most part—moderation and balance.

Abba Zosimas used to say: "We have lost our sense of balance."[21]

The key was discernment; that was the "royal way."

Abba Joseph asked Abba Poemen: "How should one fast?" Abba Poemen said to him: "For my part, I think it better that one should eat every day, but only a little, so as not to be satisfied." Abba Joseph said to him: "When you were younger, did you not fast two days at a time, Abba?" The old man said: "Yes, even for three days and four and the whole week. The Fathers tried all this out as they were able, and they found it preferable to eat every day, but just a small amount. They have left us this royal way, which is light."

Abba Poemen also said: "Everything that goes to excess comes from the demons."[22]

20. Poemen 8.
21. *Reflections* XI, e.
22. Poemen 31 and 129.

Not all of the desert elders taught or practiced this. There were exceptions to the rule, although often these would be from representatives of the later monastic generations:

> It was said of Abba Isaac that he ate the ashes from the incense offering with his bread.[23]

Sometimes, when reading such statements in the *Sayings*, it is helpful to remember that the Desert Fathers and Mothers are not describing the pretty result of a long ascetic struggle. Rather, they are detailing the long and painful process itself that leads to the final result.

---

23. Isaac of Cellia 6. See also Eulogius 1.

# Spiritual Guidance along the Way

If the bad news is that the way is painful, the good news is that we are not to travel this way alone. The desert elders are convinced that we cannot address our passions, we cannot know our heart, without the presence of at least one other person. We require a counselor, an advisor, a guide. We need someone to consult, someone with whom to share. We are supposed to reveal our inner thoughts, share our every thought—including, and perhaps highlighting the darker side—honestly and verbally.

> A brother said to Abba Poemen: "Why should I not be free to live without manifesting my thoughts to the old men?" The old man replied: "Abba John the Dwarf said: 'The enemy rejoices over nothing so much as over those who do not manifest their thoughts.'"[1]

Indeed, there is something refreshing and even redeeming in simply sharing verbally. There is a healing aspect to the simple act of expressing our thoughts and feelings. We are remarkably related to and dependent upon one another. Doing by sharing is always better than going alone. Nothing is left to whim in the Egyptian desert; everything is a part of the whole. For the founder of the desert way, this includes sharing the slightest details:

> Abba Antony said this: "If he is able to, a monk ought to tell his elders confidently how many steps he takes and how many drops of water he drinks in his cell, in case he is in error about these."[2]

In "telling our elders confidently" all that we do, which is another way of saying "confessing to our spiritual guide" all that we feel, we gradually learn and grow. Such obedience through personal direction and consultation is yet another way of silence; it is a

1. Poemen 101.
2. Antony 38.

way of slowing down in a fast-moving world in order to pay attention to every detail of our life and our world. Ultimately, what we learn through attention and what we grow in through direction is again the way of love. *Counseling is the first step toward community.* Obedience is a celebration of unity in daily chores and personal thoughts. In admitting to another what we think, what we do and what we feel, we learn to be forgiven and loved.

> Often the blessed Abba Zosimas would say: "We human beings do not know how to be loved and how to be honored."[3]

Yet, still more importantly, we learn also to forgive and love. Spiritual direction is the safeguard of all that happens in the desert and the measure of all that occurs in the spiritual life.

The spiritual elder—or the *abba*, the *amma*—is the one who has journeyed along the way of the desert. The spiritual director is the one who has survived the desert and, therefore, can speak both with confidence and with compassion, with authority and with charity alike. The spiritual elder can provide guidelines against the pitfalls and pointers to places of refreshment. The way, of course, always remains personal; each of us follows a way that we carve out for ourselves. Yet the journey is social; we travel together with a sense of community.

In this journey, the spiritual guide should be as dry as the desert. The elder should be characterized by discernment, which surely also includes the ability to diagnose. This comes from experience, but not necessarily with age.

> Abba Joseph said: "While we were sitting with Abba Poemen, he mentioned Abba Agathon as being an abba, and we said to him: "He is very young; why do you call him 'Abba'?" Abba Poemen replied: "Because his speech makes him worthy of being called abba."[4]

The *abba* or *amma* should never block the way; they should never steal the limelight. They should never stand out, but always stand beside us. In fact, they should be characterized by few words, by the same golden virtues of the desert: namely, silence and fasting. The

---

3. *Reflections* XI, e.
4. Poemen 61.

spiritual director is not a tourist-guide, but a fellow traveler on the same path.

> A brother said to Abba Theodore: "Speak a word to me, for I am perishing." Sorrowfully, the old man said to him: "I am myself in danger. So what can I say to you?"[5]

The danger is that we often tend to romanticize matters of spiritual direction. We may idealize the process, expecting it to solve our problems. Or else, we may idolize a certain elder, seeking final—even absolute—answers in their words or their actions. In the Egyptian desert, there was no room for such cult-figures. What preserves the authenticity of spiritual direction in the desert is the unrelenting sense of accountability and responsibility. No one set himself or herself up as an authority. Abandonment to another in obedience was the only avenue toward grace; but it was expected of everyone, elders and novices alike! *Obedience was a circle* that involved and included everyone; to be excluded from this circle of obedience was to create a vicious cycle of domination.

> Abba Mios of Belos said: "Obedience responds to obedience!"[6]

This is perhaps also one of the reasons why ordination to the priesthood was avoided within monastic groups and communities. It was regarded as a source for ambition and clericalism.

> Peter, priest of Dios, ought to have stood in front when he prayed with others, because he was a priest. Yet, because of his humility, he stood behind.[7]

The desert seemed to place everyone on an identical level, on an equal footing in terms of accountability before one another and before God. Obedience was the great leveler, the ultimate equalizer or the common denominator in the desert. It served not so much to establish a hierarchical structure, but rather to unite the community. Everyone was bound, committed and accountable to the rule of obedience. Furthermore, the desert elders had an aversion to any form of attachment, be this material or personal. As we shall see below, it was detachment that was prized in the desert. If the

5. Theodore of Pherme 20.
6. Mios 1.
7. Peter of Dios 1.

Desert Fathers and Mothers became beacons of spiritual direction, it was because they first rejected human structures of power.

> Amma Theodora said that a teacher ought to be a stranger to the desire for domination, vainglory and pride. One should not be able to fool that person by flattery, nor blind that person by gifts. . . . Rather, the teacher should be patient, gentle and humble as far as possible; the teacher must also be tested and be without favoritism, full of concern for others, and a lover of souls.[8]

An ages-long spiritual heritage, of which they comprised only a part, taught them that alongside the more institutional lines of "apostolic succession" there was also a complementary inspirational element of "spiritual succession." This is why they did not establish regulations or write down fixed rules. The only rule was that there were no hard rules. Flexibility was the sole rule of the desert.

> A brother asked Abba Poemen: "Some brothers live with me; should I be in charge of them?" The old man said to him: "No, just work first and foremost. And if they want to live like you, then they will see to it themselves." The brother said to him: "But it is they themselves, Father, who want me to be in charge of them." The old man replied: "No, be their example, not their legislator."[9]

> A brother once asked Abba Sisoes to give him a word. He said: "Why do you make me speak without need? Whatever you see, do it."[10]

This was the manner in which the spiritual guides were to conduct and control themselves before their disciples. At the same time, it was the manner in which the disciples looked to and learned from their elders.

> Three Fathers used to go and visit the blessed Antony every year; two of them would discuss their thoughts and the salvation of their souls with the old man, but the third always remained silent and did not ask him anything. After a long time, Abba Antony said to him: "You often come here to see me, but you never ask me anything." And the brother replied: "It is enough for me to see you, Father."[11]

8. Theodora 5.
9. Poemen 174.
10. Sisoes 45. See also Isaac of Cellia 2.
11. Antony 27.

It cannot always have been easy to avoid offering precepts. Nor could it at all times have been possible to avoid friction in personal relationships. Unfortunately, in the collecting and editing of *The Sayings of the Desert Fathers,* much of that original process and tension has been wiped out, leaving us simply with the final product of their wisdom. Nevertheless, every once in a while, we can gleam some of that struggle that led to their conviction about allowing space for personal growth in spiritual direction. This notion of "allowing or sharing space" is the literal meaning of the Greek term *syn-chore-sis* as well as its English equivalent translation "for-give-ness."

As you read the following story, you will notice how much the elder strives to avoid giving a clear directive to the brother who asks for advice:

> A brother questioned Abba Poemen, saying: "I am losing my soul through living near my abba. Should I go on living with him?"

This question strikes at the very core of spiritual direction, which itself lies at the very heart of the desert way. What happens when there is a disagreement between elder and disciple? What happens when the solution itself becomes a problem?

> The old man knew that he was finding it harmful to stay with the abba. So he said to him: "Stay, if you want." The brother left him and stayed on there. He came back again and said: "I am losing my soul." But again the old man did not tell him to leave. He came a third time and said: "I really cannot stay there any longer. I am leaving." Then Abba Poemen said to him: "Now you have truly been healed. Go, and do not stay with him any longer."[12]

Abba Poemen struggled to exclude his own will while expanding—but not exploiting—the will of the brother. The struggle to refrain from interfering in another person's journey was yet another way of expressing respect for, and love toward, that person. This virtue is another form of renunciation. For the desert elders, detachment from everything and everyone only underlined the dignity of everything and everyone. It would have been so simple for Abba Poemen to offer advice to the brother from the first instance; it might even have saved the brother two subsequent visits to the elder. Yet, it might have proved a premature step in the

12. Poemen 189.

growth process of the brother. Instead, Abba Poemen chose to detach himself, to forego, to let go of his instinctive reaction to interfere in this sensitive process. He knew very well that spiritual direction is not the gift of a response that solves a problem, but the gift of a path that leads the disciple to be saved—to be healed and made whole.

# The Power of Detachment

Detachment (*apotage*, ἀποταγή), therefore, is an ongoing lesson learned over years in the desert. In one way, it is the first step of monastic renunciation or of the flight to the desert.

> Abba Arsenius prayed to God in these words: "Lord, lead me in the way of salvation." And a voice came, saying to him: "Arsenius, flee from people and you will be saved."[1]

Yet, detachment is more than merely spatial or material.

> Abba Zosimas always like to say: "It is not possessing something that is harmful, but being attached to it."[2]

Detachment is not the inability to focus on things, material or other; it is the spiritual capacity to focus on all things, material and other, without attachment. It is primarily something spiritual; it is an attitude of life. And in this respect, detachment is ongoing, requiring continual refinement.

There are stages in the way of detachment, just as there are steps in the ladder of spiritual life.[3] Perhaps we should look at detachment not so much as the first stage, but as *a series of stages of refinement*. There are, in fact, a number of successive detachments that one undergoes in the desert. Detachment resembles the shedding of a number of coats of skin, until our senses are sharpened, or until "our inner vision becomes keen."[4] When we learn what to let go of, we also learn what it is that is worth holding on to.

1. Arsenius 1.
2. *Reflections* I, b and XV, d.
3. *The Ladder of Divine Ascent* is the title of a brilliant seventh-century monastic text written by John Climacus, former hermit and later abbot of the monastery on Mount Sinai. See the translation by C. Luibheid and N. Russell in *The Classics of Western Spirituality* series (New York: Paulist Press, 1982).
4. Doulas 1.

Abba Zosimas said: "In time, through neglect, we lose even the little fervor that we suppose that we have in our ascetic renunciation. We become attached to useless, insignificant and entirely worthless matters, substituting these for the love of God and neighbor, appropriating material things as if they were our own or as if we had not received them from God. 'What do you have that you did not receive? And if you received it, then why do you boast as if it were not a gift?'" (1 Cor.4.7)[5]

Think of it in this way: it is simply not possible to share something precious or even to hold a lover's hand, when we keep our fists clenched, holding tightly onto something. The purpose of monastic detachment is not to live apart from the social world, but to learn how to live in the world as a part of society.

One day Abba Longinus questioned Abba Lucius about three thoughts, saying first: "I want to go into exile." The old man said: "If you cannot control your tongue, you will not be in exile anywhere. Therefore, control your tongue here, and you will be in exile." Next he said to him: "I wish to fast." The old man replied: "If you bend your neck like a rope or bulrush, that is not the fast that God will accept; but rather, control your evil thoughts." He said to him the third time: "I wish to flee from people." The old man responded: "If you have not first of all lived rightly with people, then you will not be able to live properly in solitude either."[6]

Detachment, then, makes us neither dependent nor detached from people. Instead, it makes us more transparent, allowing for truth and sincerity in personal relationships.

Abba Agathon said: "Under no circumstances should a monk let his conscience accuse him of anything."

He also said: "I have never gone to sleep with a grievance against anyone. And, as far as I could, I have never let anyone go to sleep with a grievance against me."[7]

Detachment implies sensitivity in actions, in words, and even in gestures.

5. *Reflections* X, c.
6. Longinus 1.
7. Agathon 2 and 4.

Abba Isaiah said: "When someone wishes to render evil for evil, that person can cause harm to another's soul even by a single nod of the head."[8]

This attitude extends also beyond one's connection with other people to one's relationship to material things.

The same Abba Agathon was walking with his disciples. One of them, on finding a small green pea on the road, said to the old man: "Father, may I take it?" The old man, looking at him with astonishment, replied: "Was it you that put it there?" "No," said the brother. "How then," continued the old man, "can you take up something, which you did not put down?"[9]

The detachment that is recommended here is a form of letting go. We are to let go of our actions, of our statements, and finally of our very existence. The aim of letting go of our actions is the learning of the prayer, which is the starting-point and ending-point of all action.

Abba Nilus said: "Everything that you do in revenge against a brother who has harmed you will come back to your mind at the time of prayer."

He also said: "Whatever you have endured out of love of wisdom will bear fruit for you at the time of prayer."[10]

In prayer (*proseuche*, προσευχή), we are literally letting go; renouncing and refining so many images and so much information that veil our relationship to God and weigh down on the soul. By letting go, we learn to pray spontaneously, a gift that children seem to have innately, but which takes a lifetime to recover as adults.

In prayer, the way of silence and the way of service coincide.

Abba Poemen said: "If three people meet, of whom the first fully preserves interior peace, and the second gives thanks to God in illness, and the third serves with a pure mind, these three are doing the same work."[11]

Work is not separated from prayer.

8. Isaiah 8.
9. Agathon 11. See also Agathon 12.
10. Nilus 1 and 5.
11. Poemen 29.

> It was said of Abba Apollo, that he had a disciple named Isaac, perfectly trained in all good works and in the gift of ceaseless prayer. . . . He used to say that all things are good in their proper time, "for there is a time for everything."[12] (Cf. Eccles. 3.1-8)

Instead, prayer frees us for carefree service of others, where we are no longer conditioned by the burden of necessity but always prepared for the novelty of grace's surprise.

Just as *prayer conditions our works, silence conditions our words.* We have already discussed the importance of silence. It too is another form of freedom and detachment.

> Abba Theophilus, the archbishop [of Alexandria], came to Scetis one day. The brothers who were assembled said to Abba Pambo: "Say something to the archbishop, so that he may be edified." The old man said to them: "If he is not edified by my silence, then he will not be edified by my speech."[13]

> Abba Poemen said: "If you are silent, you will have peace wherever you live."[14]

> One day, some elders came to see Abba Antony. Among them was Abba Joseph. Wanting to test them, Abba Antony suggested a text from the Scriptures. Beginning with the youngest, he asked them what it meant. Each gave an opinion, as he was able. But to each one the old man said: "You have not understood it." Last of all, he said to Abba Joseph: "How would you explain this saying?" Joseph replied: "I do not know." Then Abba Antony said: "Indeed, Abba Joseph has found the way. For he has said: 'I do not know.'"[15]

Indeed, silence can even heal the sick![16] On the other hand, words can also hurt. Perhaps this is because words often conceal hypocrisy rather than authenticity; and they may sometimes exclude rather than embrace.

> Abba Poemen said that a brother who lived with some other brothers asked Abba Bessarion: "What ought I to do?" The old man said to him: "Keep silence, and do not be always comparing yourself with others."[17]

12. Isaac the Theban 2.
13. Theophilus 1.
14. Poemen 84.
15. Antony 17.
16. Nisteros the Cenobite 1.
17. Poemen 79.

Finally, detachment signifies letting go of our very being. It is a sign of humility, which in the desert is treasured "above all virtues."[18]

> Amma Theodora said that neither asceticism, nor vigils, nor any kind of suffering are able to save. Only true humility can do that. There was a hermit who was able to banish the demons. And he asked them: "What makes you go away? Is it fasting?" They replied: "We do not eat or drink." "Is it vigils?" They said: "We do not sleep." "Then what power sends you away?" They replied: "Nothing can overcome us except humility alone." Amma Theodora said: "Do you see how humility is victorious over the demons?"[19]

Humility looks to shift the focus of oneself as the center of the world and to place oneself in the service of others.

> Abba Poemen said: "Do not do your own will; rather, humble yourself before your neighbor."[20]

> Abba Or gave this advice: "Whenever you want to subdue your high and proud thoughts, examine your conscience carefully: Have you loved your enemies and been kind to them in their misfortunes?"[21]

The humble person is always satisfied, always shares, always gives, always gives thanks. In fact, one learns to give thanks even for misfortunes.

> The blessed Abba Zosimas added: "It is true that one ought to give thanks for these things and, if one is indeed filled with passions, to regard such people [who bring us misfortune] as doctors who heal the wounds of the soul; and if one is dispassionate, one should regard them as benefactors who procure for us the heavenly kingdom."[22]

Gratitude (*eucharistia*) is the vessel that contains grace (*charis*); it is the human expression of a divine experience defined as learning to share.

18. John the Dwarf 22.
19. Theodora 6. See also Antony 7.
20. Poemen 158.
21. Or 11.
22. Abba Zosimas, *Reflections* XII, a. See also Abba Dorotheus, *Letter IX*, 194 (p. 516).

# Education and Formation

Giving and sharing are of the essence of the desert. Often, we think of the Desert Fathers and Mothers as sources of factual information. Rather, we should look at them as sources of spiritual formation. The desert had its own system of education; it was its own school of thought.

> Someone said to the blessed Arsenius: "How is it that we, with all our education and our wide knowledge get nowhere, while these Egyptian peasants acquire so many virtues?" Abba Arsenius replied: "We indeed get nothing from our secular education, but these Egyptian peasants acquire the virtues by hard work."[1]

The education of these "Egyptian peasants" was transformational and not merely informational.

> A brother came to Abba Theodore and spent three days begging him to say a word to him, but without getting a single reply. So, he went away aggrieved. Then the old man's disciple asked him: "Abba, why did you not say a word to him? See how he has gone away grieved?" The old man said: "I did not speak to him because he is a trafficker who seeks to glorify himself through the words of others."[2]

Talking about subjects that truly mattered was not always easy, even in the desert, and especially for those of the elders who were more intellectual.

> Abba Evagrius said: "Once when I was talking to some brothers on a helpful topic, they were overcome by sleep so deep, that they could not even move their eyelids any longer. Then, wishing to show them the power of the devil, I introduced a trivial subject of conversation. And immediately, they woke up, full of joy!"[3]

1. Arsenius 5.
2. Theodore of Pherme 3.
3. Evagrius 6.

As *The Sayings of the Desert Fathers* moved from an oral tradition to a written culture, they also lost a certain amount of their original spontaneity and imaginative charisma. Yet, in general, *the desert produced healers, not thinkers.* It cultivated the heart, not letters. It sought to quench a thirst of the soul, and not merely a curiosity of the mind. The desert was a place of inner work and of personal experience.

> A brother came to Abba Theodore and began to converse with him about things he had never yet put into practice. So the old man said to him: "You have not yet found a ship nor put your cargo aboard it; yet before you have sailed, you have already arrived at the city! Do the work first; and then you will have the speed you are making now."[4]

> Abba Cassian said: "I have never done my own will, nor taught anything, which I have not previously carried out myself."[5]

> Abba Abraham told the story of a man of Scetis who was a scribe and did not eat bread. A brother came to beg him to copy a book. The old man, whose spirit was engaged in contemplation, wrote, omitting some phrases and with no punctuation. The brother, taking the book and wishing to punctuate it, noticed that words were missing. So he said to the old man: "Abba, there are some phrases missing." The old man replied: "Go, practice first that which is written; then come back and I will write the rest."[6]

The point of departure in the desert was learning and not teaching; the priority was discipline and not the making of disciples.

> Abba Poemen said: "Instructing one's neighbor is for the person who is whole and without passions. For what is the use of building the house of another, while destroying one's own?"[7]

> Abba Macarius said: "Do not lose yourself in order to save another."[8]

The Coptic monks of the desert knew only a single word and a single struggle for designating both the mind and the heart. We

4. Theodore of Pherme 9.
5. Cassian 5.
6. Abraham 3.
7. Poemen 127.
8. Macarius 17.

tend to separate the mind from the heart. We like to fill the mind; yet, we forget the heart. Or else, we fill the heart with information that should fill the mind. Nevertheless, the two work differently: the mind learns; the heart knows. The mind is educated; the heart believes. The mind is intellectual, speculative; it reads and speaks. The heart is intuitive, mystical; it grows in silence. The two should be held together; and they should be brought together in the presence of God.

It is not that secular education was unacceptable to the desert elders. Indeed, many of them were lettered: Arsenius, Basil, Evagrius, and Cassian. It is simply that secular education always remains insufficient without an ascetic depth; it is unfulfilled without the spiritual content. The only degree that counted in the desert was the degree to which one was humbled, even effaced, in order to reveal the presence and grace of God.

"Fathers of the solitary life"
St. Paul of Thebes (*left*) and St. Antony of Egypt (*right*)
Coptic icons, 18th century

*I*

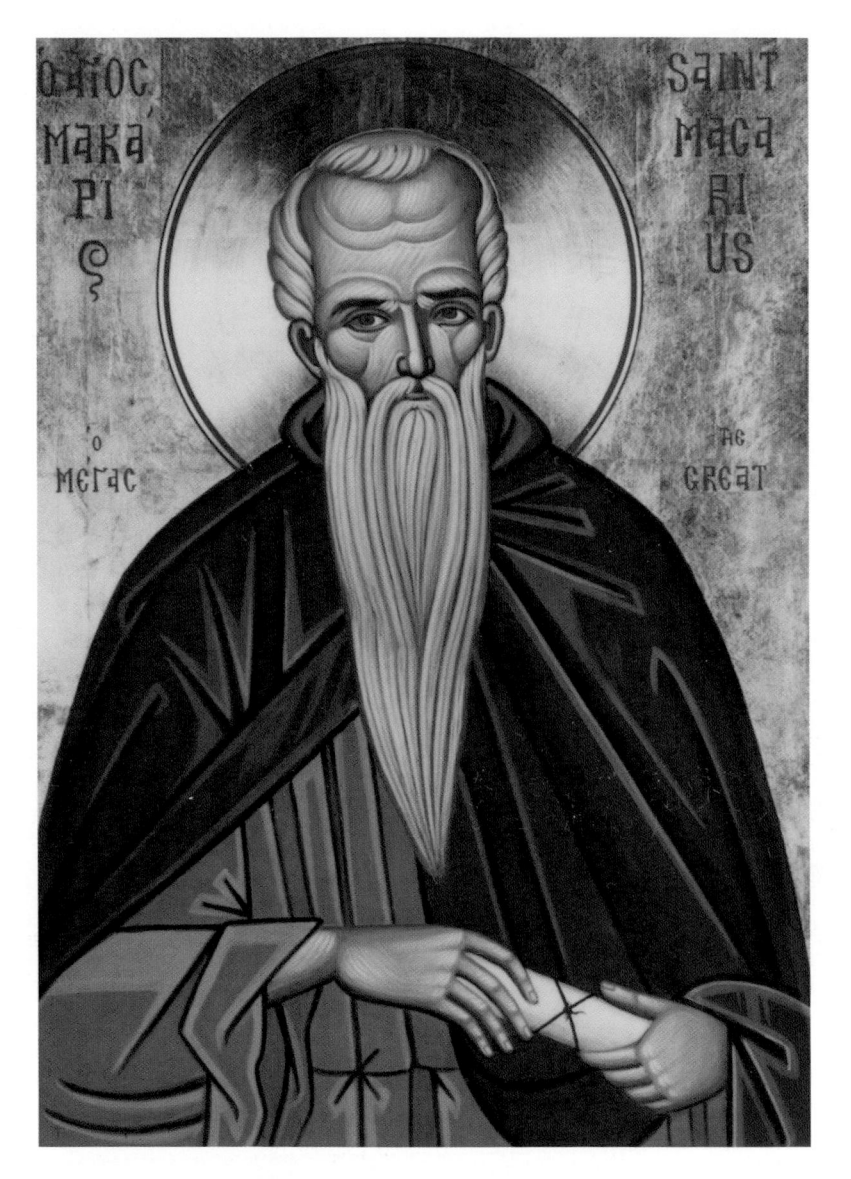

"Like a god upon this earth"
Abba Macarius of Egypt
Holy Transfiguration Monastery, Boston

"The soft-natured robber"
Abba Moses the Ethiopian
Holy Transfiguration Monastery, Boston

"Gentleness, patience, and moderation"
Amma Syncletica
Holy Transfiguration Monastery, Boston

"The humble noble"
Abba Arsenius the Great
Holy Transfiguration Monastery, Boston

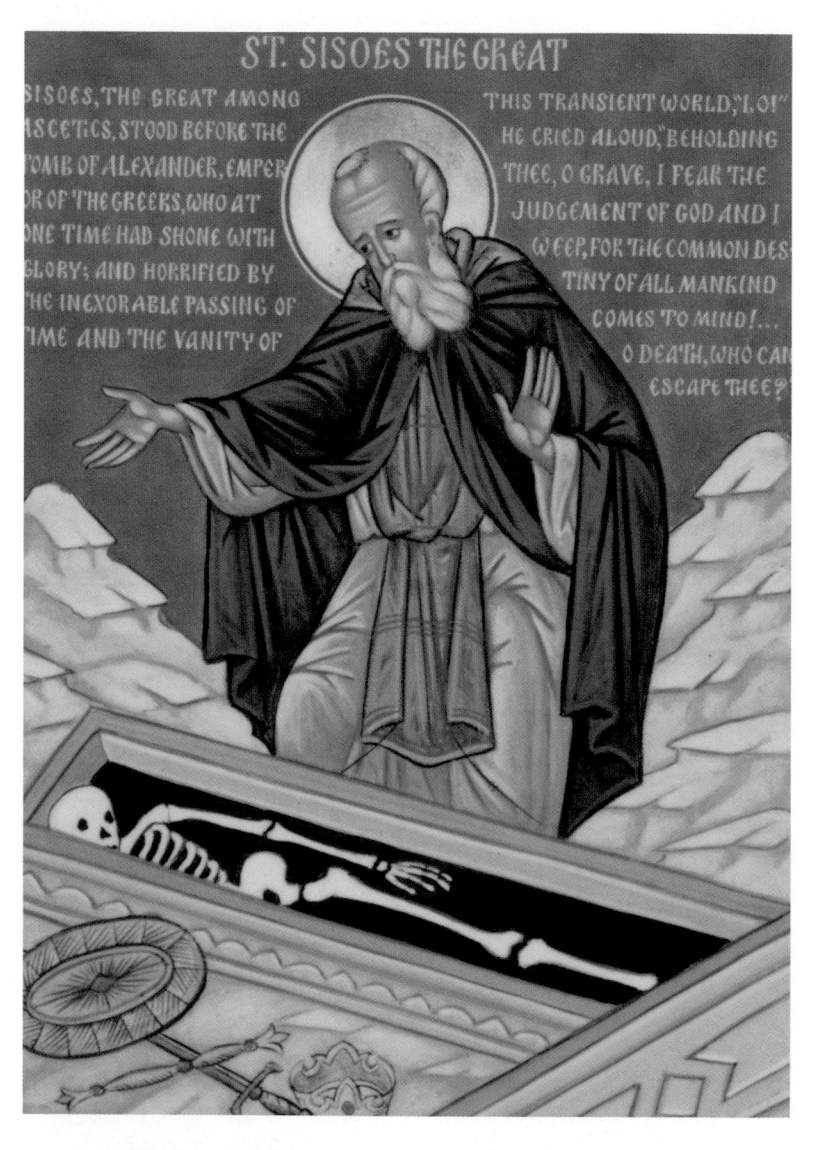

"Patience, silence, and remembrance of death"
Abba Sisoes the Great
Holy Transfiguration Monastery, Boston

"The circle of obedience"
Mary of Egypt receiving communion from Zosimas
Icon from Asia Minor, 18th century

"Founder of the common life"
St. Pachomius the Great
Bulgarian icon

"The desert became a city"
Monastery of St. George
Wadi el Qelt

"It was there that Moses saw God"
Monastery of St. Catherine
Mount Sinai

"A powerful symbol of the inner space,
where we yearn for God"
Grand Canyon, Arizona

"In caves and in holes in the ground"
Hebrews 11.38
Entry to Antony's cave, Egypt

"The legacy of the desert"
Entrances to hermit cells in Cappadocia

"Between heaven and earth"
The Monastery of Roussano
Meteora, Greece

"They wandered in deserts and mountains"
Hebrews 11.38
*Top*: Some of the caves of Qumran in the wilderness of Judah
*Bottom*: The Lavra of St. Saba in the desert of Judah, Palestine

"Birthplace of the desert tradition"
Remains of hermitages in Kellia

# Solitude and Charity

Such, then, is the methodology with which we should appreciate some of the more difficult aspects of life in the desert. One of the first questions that arises as we read the *Apophthegmata* and consider these elders is the elitism of their experience? Is it, for example, selfish to withdraw into the desert when there appears to be so much suffering in the world? Are the Desert Fathers and Mothers anti-social figures of fourth-century Egypt? Certainly, there are abundant passages in the *Sayings* to affirm this description of them.

> Abba Sisoes was sitting in his cell one day, when his disciple knocked on the door to ask the old man something. Abba Sisoes shouted out to him saying: "Go away, Abraham, do not come in. From now on, I have no time for the things of this world."[1]

At the same time, however, it is in these very *Sayings* that one encounters the illuminating words of Abba Antony:

> Abba Antony said: "Our life and our death is with our neighbor. If we gain our brother, then we have gained God; but if we scandalize our brother, then we have sinned against Christ."[2]

How can someone affirm this after spending most of his life in solitude?

The simple answer, then, to the question that we posed concerning elitism is that the way of the desert is not a selfish way, so long as everyone else is also traveling the same journey. If each of us, as contemporary readers of these ancient *Sayings* in the twenty-first century, has embarked upon the stage of the desert, then we will appreciate the un-selfishness of the elders that lived there in the fourth century.

1. Sisoes 27.
2. Antony 9.

Nevertheless, if we remain outside of the desert process, then their way will surely appear selfish. Remember that everyone is called to go through the desert. Nonetheless, no one needs to stay in the desert forever. Even Antony came outside the desert on two occasions in his life: the first time, in order to support the martyrs; and the second time in order to support his friend Athanasius in his fourth-century theological argumentation against Arius. In fact, perhaps more importantly, Antony also moved out of his desert spiritually as well as geographically, by allowing other disciples to gather around him and look to him as their spiritual director. Perhaps it would be more appropriate to say that Antony never really left the desert, even when he set foot outside of the desert. For, Antony is always speaking *from the desert*; his every word and action are coming *from the desert*.

In any case, there is something sincerely presumptuous and spiritually misleading about imagining that the silence of the desert somehow transcends service in the world. Moreover, Antony and his colleagues never deny the world; instead, they are very understanding toward the world.

> A hunter in the desert once saw Abba Antony enjoying himself with the brothers, and he was shocked. Wanting to show him that it was necessary sometimes to meet the needs of the brothers, the old man said to the hunter: "Put an arrow in your bow and shoot it." So he did. The old man then said: "Shoot another arrow." And he did so. Then the old man said: "Shoot yet again." But the hunter replied: "If I bend my bow so much I will break it." Then Antony said to him: "It is the same with the work of God. If we stretch the brothers beyond their measure, they will soon break. Sometimes it is necessary to come down to meet their needs."[3]

Yet, there is another perspective from which to consider this question about selfishness. It may be that we are in fact called to be more selfish in the spiritual life. This may sound strange, but perhaps we ought to set aside a time and a place where we do nothing else at all but address the passions of the soul and meditate on God. It may be that we should *take time out for ourselves and for God* in the same way as we do—quite naturally, and without ever considering that this is in any way selfish—to eat and rest and be entertained.

3. Antony 13.

The truth is that we are no good to others or to ourselves if we avoid or miss this stage of the desert. The Desert Fathers and Mothers emphasize the need for an integrated self. Remember the words of Abba Alonius: we must, he claimed, be totally alone with God and with ourselves in order to rebuild and reshape ourselves.[4]

We must never use love and service as excuses to avoid the inner work of transformation. All of us—and especially those in the caring professions—should take time out for ourselves in retreat, for our friends in relaxation, and for God in prayer. The Desert Fathers and Mothers teach us that love is not an outpouring of the self that resembles the water that is poured into sand or else into a bucket with holes. Prayer, even the most intense form of solitary meditation, is deeply connected to our ability to relate to others. Anthony Bloom, the author of a foreword to the alphabetical collection of *Sayings*, writes elsewhere about the way that we can manage time in order to "retreat" to the desert of the heart in a tense and busy modern life. He speaks of "being completely in the present moment." He recommends that we try to find a time, when we have absolutely nothing to do, when nothing pulls us either backward or forward.

> Say: "I am seated, I am doing nothing, I will do nothing for five minutes," and then relax, and continually throughout this time . . . realize, "I am here in the presence of God, in my own presence and in the presence of all the furniture that is around me, just still, moving nowhere now with myself."

So, we are just to sit with ourselves. This in itself is difficult, an onerous labor. Bloom continues in language that echoes Abba Alonius in a striking manner:

> Try an experiment and you will see, you will discover a number of useful things on the way. Try to find time to stay alone with yourself; shut the door and settle down in your room at a moment when you have nothing else to do. Say: "I am now with myself," and just sit with yourself.

> After an amazingly short time, you will most likely feel bored. This teaches us one very useful thing. It gives us insight into the fact that, if after ten minutes of being alone with ourselves, we feel like

4. Alonius 1 and 2.

that, it is no wonder that others should feel equally bored! . . . This is really a very dramatic discovery. We are completely empty, we do not act from within ourselves but accept as our life a life which is actually fed in from outside; we are used to things happening which compel us to do other things. How seldom can we live simply by means of the depth and the richness we assume that there is within ourselves.[5]

The intensity of retreat and silence are an opening up into the integrity of life and caring, as well as into the community of love and sharing.

Abba Apollo said: "When you see your brother, you have seen the Lord your God."[6]

5. *Beginning to Pray* (New York: Paulist Press, 1970), pp. 85 and 67-68.
6. Apollo 3.

# THIRTEEN

# The Desert and the Body

If the desert elders are not selfish, if they are simply men and women who are learning the hard lesson of sharing, are they perhaps opponents of the flesh? Do they hate the body? We have already seen how it is not difficult to find harsh statements about the passions and against the body in the *Sayings*. Yet, we have also seen how we should be careful to ask what these statements actually imply. Are the elders speaking of subduing the body or the passions? Are they referring to the destruction of the passions or to their transformation?

It appears that the desert treats the body harshly; but in fact, the emphasis is on shedding the excess layers, on getting rid of the dead layers, which they define as "flesh." Detachment is a way of renouncing excess baggage and of traveling light. And the truth is that *we can always manage with less than we have*; indeed, we can often manage with a lot less than we would dare to imagine. Even while claiming that the entire world belongs to God, the desert elders strive no longer to depend on material possessions. Their struggle is not to become centered on the world; it is to establish another order and focus, where the entire world is centered on God.

When Antony of Egypt emerged from complete withdrawal into his beloved "inner mountain," we read that:

> His friends were amazed to see that his body had maintained its former condition, being neither too puffed up from lack of exercise nor too emaciated from fasting and warfare against the demons. He was just as they had known him prior to his retreat into the desert. . . . He was altogether balanced, just as one guided by reason and abiding in a natural state.[1]

1. *Life of Antony*, ch. 14.

Although Athanasius' biography of Antony may be a somewhat idealized account, it is nevertheless reliable and historical. Notice, then, the words used by Athanasius to describe Antony: "former condition," "just as they had known him," "altogether balanced," "guided by reason," and "natural state." This is not what we have come to accept as the attitude, for instance, of Plotinus (c.204-270) who was ashamed of his body, or of the Gnostics who hated the body. In fact, as we have seen, Antony went on to live for over one hundred years. Athanasius even offers us further details:

> His eyes were undimmed and quite sound; and he saw clearly. He had lost none of his teeth; they had simply become worn down to the gums because of the old man's great age. He remained strong in both feet and hands.[2]

Clearly, Antony's austere asceticism did not impair his health. In fact, quite the contrary: it seems to have enhanced it.

The ascetic's treatment of the body appears negative to us because we have overloaded the body with far too much. The change, therefore, as we move from our lifestyle to Antony's, seems so overwhelming and enormous that it creates a sense of vertigo within us. Our bodies go through "withdrawal symptoms" when confronted with the radical withdrawal of Antony into the desert. Our culture teaches us that the more we have, the better we are; Antony's taught him that the less he had, the more he was! We are carrying so much baggage, so many preoccupations and concerns, such great loads that walking freely with God looks frightening, unfamiliar and painful. And our natural response is to resist change; it simply seems crazy to us.

> Abba Antony said: "A time is coming when people will go insane. And when they see someone who is not insane, they will attack that person saying: 'You are crazy; you are not like us.'"[3]

---

2. *Ibid.*, ch. 93.
3. Antony 25. On the importance of possessing material things with detachment, see also Abba Zosimas, *Reflections* XV, d.

# The Desert and the Environment

If Antony and the other desert elders are not against society or against the body, might we criticize them for overlooking the natural and aesthetic beauty of the creation through their austere practice and harsh discipline? What is the relationship that the desert dwellers had with their environment and with the animals? In renouncing the world, the Desert Fathers and Mothers did not overlook the world; in fact, they enjoyed a new awareness of everything that is in the world—human, animal, and natural.

In the *Life of Antony*, we are told that Abba Antony saw the desert for the first time "and loved it."[1] The desert was home for Antony and the other elders who lived there. It was there that they experienced their sense of communion with the earth as well as their communion with God. It is there that they also experienced a sense of continuity with the land and with their past.

> Abba John the Eunuch said: "Let us imitate our Fathers. For they lived in this place with much austerity and peace."[2]

The desert was a positive and a beautiful place, where those who so desired were able to see God, to hear God, and to live with God. Detachment also meant that the Desert Fathers and Mothers became as nothing, much like the sand of the desert that surrounded them. Yet, detachment further implied a sense of becoming one with the environment. Their *holiness was part and parcel of a sense of wholeness*. If at-one-ment with their neighbor was of the essence of desert spirituality, so too was at-tune-ment to their environment, to the world, and to God.

1. Chapter 50.
2. John the Eunuch 4.

Abba Antony said: "Renounce this life, so that you may be alive to God!"[3]

Abba John the Eunuch said: "My children, let us not pollute this place, since our Fathers have previously cleansed it from demons."[4]

The desert was a place to be admired for its wonderfulness and boundlessness. "Admired," says the *Life of Antony*, but not "adored"[5]; one was to wonder at, but not worship, the beauty of the desert. Worship was due to God alone as author and creator of the world. Awareness of the natural beauty of the world leads to awe before the divine beauty of God. The same conviction informs the second part of our response to the question about desert attitudes to the surrounding natural and animal environment.

When it comes to relating to the animals, there is an abundance of information about the connection that the desert dwellers enjoyed with their co-inhabitants of the desert.

One of the Fathers used to tell of a certain Abba Paul, from lower Egypt, who lived in the Thebaid. He used to take various kinds of snakes in his hands. . . . The brothers made a prostration before him, asking: "Tell us what you have done to receive this grace." He said: "Forgive me, Fathers, but if someone acquires purity, then everything is in submission to that person, just as it was for Adam when he was in paradise before the transgression of the commandment."[6]

Abba Antony also said: "Obedience with abstinence gives people authority even over wild beasts."[7]

Antony knew the truth of this statement. He had persuaded the animals in his region to live at peace with him and no longer to disturb him.[8] In fact, the notion of being like Adam, before he fell from the graceful condition he enjoyed in paradise, is the ideal to which the desert elders aspired.

3. Antony 33.
4. John the Eunuch 5.
5. Chapter 76.
6. Paul 1.
7. Antony 36.
8. *Life of Antony*, ch. 50.

They said of Abba Pambo that his face was like that of Moses, who received the image of the glory of Adam when his face shone. Pambo's face also shone like lightening, and he was like a king sitting on a throne. It was the same with Abba Silvanus and Abba Sisoes.[9]

One finds such a relationship with creation and with animals throughout the history of spiritual heroes. It is *a relationship that transcends place*: we find it in the writing of Abba Isaac the Syrian (7th century) as well as in the life of St. Francis of Assisi (1181-1226). It is also *a relationship that transcends time*: we notice it in the hermits of early Palestine as well as in the nineteenth-century life of St. Seraphim of Sarov (1759-1833). Yet, this is more than a mere emotional attachment to animals. It may be helpful to recall once again the emphasis on detachment in the desert. The connection with land and animals is neither superficial nor sentimental; it is deeply theological. It stems from the inner conviction of these hermits that God created this world; and this implies that God loves and cares for the world, as well as for all that is in the world, both animate and inanimate. The desert elders were, in the most intense and intimate manner, "materialists." Everything—including simple matter—really mattered! In God's eyes, both animals and sand dunes are of importance and have their place; in Heaven, birds and trees are not excluded.

If the purpose of fleeing to the desert was to reestablish a lost order, then a reconciliation with all of the creation and the reconnection of this entire world with God was critical. These elders may sometimes appear eccentric; but *eccentricity means moving the center, recentering the world on God*. The world becomes a wasteland unless it, too, comes alive in an authentic human being, who in turn becomes the eyes of the world and its conscience. Therefore, if we miss the stage of the desert, it may be that we shall also cause a split between the world and ourselves; ultimately, we are causing a split within ourselves. As the saying goes: if you don't go within, then you go without. When we neglect the world of the spirit, then we also end up neglecting the spirit of the world; and when we disregard the world of our soul, we in fact end up ignoring the soul of the world.

9. Pambo 12.

# FIFTEEN

## The Desert and Gender

Theoretically, anyone could enter the desert. People from all classes, hermits of every kind of temperament, elders of any background, education, status, and virtue: they could all leave their worldly attachments and aspire to desert detachment. Ideally, the desert defied any kind of discrimination. I say ideally, because the Desert Fathers and Mothers were not always able to break with worldly forms of discrimination. It was, however, their ongoing struggle to test just how much they had moved beyond the limitations of society. It was the desert itself and its virtue that was able to overcome the world and its ignorance.

> Another day, when a council was being held in Scetis, the Fathers treated Abba Moses with contempt in order to test him, saying: "Why does this black man come among us?" When he heard this, Abba Moses kept silence. When the council was dismissed, they said to him: "Abba, did that not grieve you at all?" He said to them: "I was grieved, but I kept silence."[1]

*The desert also overlooked gender distinction, at least in theory.* Among the desert elders were men, women, and those who were eunuchs. We know, for instance, that there was a collection of stories and sayings of saintly Mothers, known as the *Meterikon*, just as there was a similar anthology for holy Fathers, called the *Paterikon*. Unfortunately, the earliest versions of the *Meterikon* did not survive, although numerous lives and legends of heroic women have been preserved. And, of course, *The Sayings of the Desert Fathers* themselves include the sayings of three Desert Mothers. Three out of the one hundred and twenty-seven elders mentioned in this alphabetical collection are in fact women: Amma Sarah, Amma Syncletica, and Amma Theodora.

1. Moses 3. See also Moses 4.

It is not surprising to find these women included in the collection of desert stories. Women were, in general, welcomed in the desert for spiritual direction and instruction. There did not seem to be a radical break from the world in terms of human presence. Examples for edification and models for imitation were also drawn from the lives of women in society.

> One day, Abba Poemen went with Abba Anoub to the district of Diolcos. Arriving at the cemetery, they saw a woman in great sorrow, weeping bitterly. Standing there, they watched her. Going a little further, they met someone and Abba Poemen asked him: "Why is this woman weeping so bitterly?" He replied: "Because her husband is dead, as well as her son and her brother." Abba Poemen told the brother: "I tell you, if a person does not mortify all one's carnal desires and acquire compunction like this, then that person cannot become a monk. Truly, the whole of this woman's life and soul are turned to compunction."[2]

Rather, the desert signified a radical break with social restrictions and discriminatory constraints of the day.

> Abba John the Eunuch said: "This is a place for asceticism, not for worldly affairs."[3]

Moving into the desert meant taking a step into the realm of freedom: freedom from slavery, freedom from obligatory subjection, freedom from exploitation, and especially freedom from possession. Generally, women in the early Christian centuries did not own themselves; they did not possess or control their lives or even their bodies. They were at the disposal of other people, normally other men, who owned them; these might include their fathers (as children), their spouses (as wives), or their lords (as servants).

In the desert, however, women were able to throw off these constraints and restrictions. In the desert, the *ammas* were able to live with a single focus, namely the heavenly kingdom, and not adhere to any earthly circumstance. And, like others both known and unknown to us in history, these women were also able to remind the men (who might otherwise have been tempted to forget!) that their goal in the desert was not to fulfill particular social roles. By struggling to exclude and overcome the conventional forms, the Desert

2. Poemen 72.
3. John the Eunuch 6.

Mothers themselves became witnesses and martyrs of another reality. Their purpose in the desert was to be detached from historical burdens and conditions that kept them chained to this world. In another age, and in the way of Christ:

> There is no longer Jew or Greek, there is no longer slave or free, there is no longer male or female, for all are one, ... heirs according to the promise (Gal. 3.28-29).

This is why their male counterparts took the women seriously. Desert Fathers would visit the Desert Mothers for counsel. Even if only three women found their way into the *Sayings*—after all, the lifestyle was still controlled by the men, and it was the men who did the preserving and the editing—nevertheless, they threw off any associations of social "weakness" expected of women and were completely identified with the men on a level beyond separation and segregation. Almost tongue in cheek, Amma Sarah was unafraid to mingle with the Desert Fathers and reminded them of their own weaknesses, insisting that they had not yet left behind worldly attachments and roles:

> Amma Sarah said to the brothers: "It is I who am a man; and you are like women!"[4]

4. Sarah 9.

# Miracles and Signs

The desert, then, was supposed to overcome earthly discriminations and limitations. What is real differed in the desert; or at least, reality acquired a different perspective. Somehow, *the order of this world was infiltrated and influenced by the order of another world.* It is no wonder, then, that the *Sayings* are literally filled with stories about miracles (*thauma*, θαῦμα), signs (*semeion*, σημεῖον) and visions (*theoria*, θεωρία or *theama*, θέαμα). There are dialogues with God and conversations with the devil; there are interventions from above that affect conditions below.

> Abba Doulas, the disciple of Abba Bessarion said: "One day, when we were walking beside the sea, I was thirsty and I said to Abba Bessarion: 'Father, I am very thirsty.' He said a prayer and told me: 'Drink some of the sea water.' The water proved sweet when I drank some. I even poured some into a leather bottle for fear of being thirsty later on. On seeing this, the old man asked me why I was taking some. I replied: 'Forgive me, it is for fear of being thirsty later on.' Then the old man said: 'God is here, God is everywhere.'"

> Another time, when Abba Bessarion had occasion to do so, he said a prayer and crossed the river Chrysoroas on foot, and then continued on his way. Filled with wonder, I asked his pardon and said: "How did your feet feel when you were walking in the water?" He replied: "I felt the water just to my heels, but the rest was dry."

> On another day, while we were going to see an old man, the sun was setting. So Abba Bessarion said this prayer: "I pray you, Lord, that the sun may stand still until we reach your servant," and this is exactly what happened.[1]

---

1. Bessarion 1-3. See also Bessarion 5; Amoun of Nitria 3; Zeno 5; Phocas 1; Gelasius 1-2; and Epiphanius 1-2.

Some of the elders had visions, and sometimes these visions were also apparent to other witnesses.

> An old man came to Abba John the Dwarf's cell and found him asleep, with an angel fanning him. Seeing this he withdrew. When Abba John awoke, he said to his disciple: "Did anyone come in while I was asleep?" He replied: "Yes, an old man." Abba John knew that this old man was his equal, and that he had seen the angel.[2]

Their prayer works miracles.

> One of the Fathers said of Abba Xoios the Theban, that one day he went to the mountain of Sinai. And when he had set out from there, a brother met him, groaning and saying: "Abba, we are in distress through lack of rain." The old man said: "Why do you not pray and ask God for some rain?" The brother replied: "We pray, we say litanies, and it does not rain." The old man said to him: "It is because you do not pray with intensity. Do you want to see that this is so?" Then he stretched his hands toward heaven in prayer and immediately it rained.[3]

Such wonders and signs are not hard evidence of saintly lives. Nor do they require scientific proof to determine whether or not they actually occurred. Within the context of life in the desert, they were quite natural phenomena. What is of importance is not so much *that* an angel stood above John the Dwarf fanning him, but *why* something like this would occur. Explaining miracles rationally is like trying to explain the existence of God logically. It is not so much that trying to make sense of God is wrong; but trying to make sense of the world without God—at least in the mind of these early Desert Fathers and Mothers—is certainly insane.

For the desert elders, miracles are paradoxical responses resulting from God's paradoxical love. They confirm God's absolute love and celebrate God's absolute freedom in a world that means everything to God as its creator. For the Desert Fathers and Mothers, creation is a miracle. The world, too, is a miracle. In fact, it is not the desert dwellers that make miracles happen; they themselves comprise miracles of God. As vessels of another grace, they remind us of the miracle of human existence. They recall the cohabitation of all the glory of God in all the frailty of humanity.

2. John the Dwarf 33. See also Ephrem 1-2.
3. Xoios 2. See also Cassian 2; Spyridon 2; Sisoes 18; and Antony 14.

The manner with which we in turn receive and respond to whatever occurs in our life—and especially the most difficult situations, the darkest moments—reflects the measure to which we too are a part of this mystery and miracle.

Miracles, then, are a part of creation and invoke our creativity. They are insights into another way of life, involving openness to mystery and welcoming the surprise of grace. We do not in fact make miracles happen; we merely witness them happening. The greatest miracles are, of course, yet to come; they await us in our life and even beyond this life. However, they appear to us even in this life and in the world, albeit "darkly, like through a glass" (1 Cor. 13.12).

# *Praying to God*

In *The Sayings of the Desert Fathers,* miracles happen through prayer (*euche,* εὐχή or *proseuche,* προσευχή). The desert offers new dimensions about our lives, about our world, and about God. In particular, the way of the desert teaches us how to pray: how to stand before God, how to speak to God, and above all how to keep silent before God. It reminds us that God is born in barrenness, where there is an absence of pride, of masks, of illusions and of false images. Paradoxically, God fulfills in emptiness. God appears when we are not too filled with other attachments and distractions, when we are not full of ourselves.

One of the lessons that we learn about prayer from the experience of the desert elders is that prayer itself is difficult. It is only grasped over time.

> The brothers asked Abba Agathon: "Among all good works, which is the virtue that requires the greatest effort?" He answered: "Forgive me, but I think that there is no greater labor than that of prayer to God. For every time a person wants to pray, one's enemies, the demons, want to prevent one from praying, for they know that it is only by turning one away from prayer that they can hinder one's journey. Whatever good works a person undertakes, if one perseveres in them, one will attain rest. But prayer is warfare to the last breath."[1]

Continual prayer does not, of course, mean that one does nothing but pray. It means that everything is included within prayer, that prayer accompanies everything that one does.

> Some of the monks who are called Euchites went to Enaton to see Abba Lucius. The old man asked them: "What is your manual labor?" They said: "We do not touch manual labor but as the Apostle says, we pray without ceasing" (Cf. 1 Thess. 5.17). The old

1. Agathon 9.

man asked them if they did not eat, and they replied that they did. So he said to them: "When you are eating, who prays for you then?" Again he asked them if they did not sleep, but they replied that they did. And he said to them: "When you are asleep, who prays for you then?" They could not find any answer to give him. He said to them: "Forgive me, but you do not act as you speak. I will show you how, while doing manual work, I pray without interruption. I sit down with God, soaking my reeds and plaiting my ropes, and I say: 'God, have mercy on me; according to your great goodness and according to the multitude of your mercies, save me from my sins.'" So he asked them if this were not prayer, and they replied that it was. Then he said to them: "So when I have spent the whole day working and praying, making thirteen pieces of money more or less, I put two pieces of money outside the door and I pay for my food with the rest of the money. The one who takes the two pieces of money prays for me when I am eating and when I am sleeping. Thus, by the grace of God, I fulfill the precept to pray without ceasing."[2]

Nevertheless, just as the desert was *a commitment to a counter-cultural way of life,* so too prayer is the realization that what matters most is not the success or the achievement or the productivity encouraged by society. Prayer is acceptance of frailty and failure—first within ourselves, and then in the world around us. When we are able to accept our brokenness, without any pretense and without any pretexts, then we are also able to embrace the brokenness of others, valuing everyone else without exception. Prayer is learning to live, without expecting to see results; it is learning to love, without hoping to see return; it is learning to be, without demanding to have. We cannot live and love and simply be, unless we are consumed by a total commitment to detachment.

Abba Joseph said to Abba Lot: "You cannot be a monk unless you become like a consuming fire."[3]

We might do well to read "human being" where Abba Joseph says "monk." It must be remembered that the monastic way of life is merely "the life according to the Gospel."[4] All people are called to

2. Lucius 1.
3. Joseph of Panephysis 6.
4. Basil, *Epistle* 207, 2. Cf. also Athanasius, *Life of Antony,* ch. 23. In this way, too, the monk is the successor of the martyr, whose sacrifice is also described as being "a martyrdom according to the Gospel." See *The Martyrdom of Polycarp,* ed.

respond to Christ's call to salvation. The circumstances of the response may vary externally, but the path is essentially one. In the spiritual life there is no sharp distinction between the monastic and the non-monastic; the monastic life is simply the Christian life, lived in a particular way. Nonetheless, every once in a while, fiery glimpses and illuminating insights reveal the line of distinction between the monastic and ourselves; every once in a while, the differences will rise to the surface in order to remind us that the monastic is a prophetic figure. Then, we remember that the ways of the Desert Fathers and Mothers are not the ways *of the world*, even if they lived *in the world*. The fire described by Abba Joseph consumed the desert elders; it is what attracted them there in the first place.

> A brother came to the cell of Abba Arsenius at Scetis. Waiting outside the door, he saw the old man entirely like a flame. (The brother was clearly worthy of this sight.) When he knocked, the old man came out and saw the brother marveling. He asked him: "Have you been knocking long? Did you see anything here?" The other answered: "No." So then they talked, and he sent the brother away.[5]

Their prayer is not always ecstatic; but it is always the fruit of long hours.

> Abba Isidore said: "When I was younger and remained in my cell, I set no limit to prayer. The whole night was for me as much the time of prayer as the day."[6]

Yet, when it comes to advising others on how to pray, the Desert Fathers and Mothers are simple and practical. Their counsel is: just pray!

> Abba Macarius was asked: "How should one pray?" The old man replied: "There is no need at all to make long discourses. It is enough to stretch out one's hands and to say: 'Lord, as you will, and as you know, have mercy.' And if the conflict grows fiercer, say: 'Lord, help!' He knows very well what we need and He shows us His mercy."[7]

J.B.Lightfoot, in *The Apostolic Fathers* (Grand Rapids MI: Baker Book House, 1956), ch. 1.
    5. Arsenius 27.
    6. Isidore the Priest 4.
    7. Macarius 19.

A brother said to Abba Antony: "Pray for me." The old man said to him: "I will have no mercy on you, nor will God have any, if you yourself do not make any effort and if you do not pray to God."[8]

Indeed, the same Antony is almost entirely undemanding when it comes to the ascetic or spiritual expectations of those who visit him. His advice could be summarized thus: do your best at what you are supposed to be doing!

The brothers came to Abba Antony and said to him: "Speak a word; how are we to be saved?" The old man said to them: "You have heard the Scriptures. That should teach you how." But they said: "Yes, but we want to hear from you too, Father." Then the old man said to them: "The Gospel says: 'If any strike you on one cheek, turn to them the other also.' (Matt. 5.39)" They said: "We cannot do that." The old man said: "Well, if you cannot offer the other cheek, at least allow one cheek to be struck." They replied: "We cannot do that either." So he said: "If you are not able to do that, then do not return evil for evil." They said: "We cannot do that either." Then the old man said to his disciple: "Prepare a little soup of corn for these people, for they are totally incapable of doing anything. If you cannot do this and cannot do that, then what can I do for you anyway? What you need is prayers."[9]

The aim is to make an effort, simply to say one's prayers. And, by saying prayers—some of the time or even much more of the time—the result is that one becomes identified with prayer all of the time. The word "pray-er" implies a living human being in the act of prayer. The Desert Fathers and Mothers themselves became like living candles of prayer.

It was said of Abba Tithoes, that when he stood up to pray, if he did not quickly lower his hands, his spirit was rapt to heaven. So if it happened that some brothers were praying with him, he hastened to lower his hands, so that his spirit would not be rapt and so that he would not pray for too long.[10]

Abba Lot went to see Abba Joseph and said to him: "Abba, as far as I can I say my little office, I fast a little, I pray and meditate, I live in peace and, again as far as I can, I purify my thoughts. What else can I do?" Then, the old man stood up and stretched his hands

8. Antony 16.
9. Antony 19.
10. Tithoes 1.

toward heaven. His fingers became like ten lamps of fire, and he said to him: "If you really want, you can become all flame."[11]

11. Joseph of Panephysis 7.

# E I G H T E E N

# *Encountering God*

In my introductory comments, I noted that the purpose of reading *The Sayings of the Desert Fathers* is to catch a glimpse of that fire and light that is characteristic of their teachings and actions. We should read these stories in order to catch alight with the same convictions that kept them aflame. When we are attentive to this spark, we shall discover certain fundamental insights about our encounter with God.

> Abba John the Dwarf gave this advice: "Watching means to sit in the cell and always be mindful of God. This is what is meant by the words: 'I was on the watch, and God came to me' (Cf. Matt. 25.36)."[1]

What exactly does it mean for God to come to us? What advice do the Desert Fathers and Mothers have to offer about encountering God? If they do not talk about their personal visions of God, then what insights do they reveal about continually seeking and ultimately seeing God?

First, the desert elders state categorically that God is not to be sought after or discovered at the end of a certain long, arduous and methodical struggle (*agon*, ἀγών, which also implies a sense of agony or anguish).

> Abba Sisoes said: "Seek God, but do not seek where God dwells."[2]

We are to *look for God not at the end, but in the very middle of the struggle.* In an earlier section, we related the story of Antony struggling fiercely against his demons, to the point of near exhaustion and death. In fact, that is not the conclusion of this striking account by Athanasius.

1. John the Dwarf 27.
2. Sisoes 40.

The Lord was not forgetful of Antony's struggle. God was at hand to assist him. So, looking up, Antony saw the roof, as it were, opened, and a ray of light descended upon him. The demons suddenly vanished, the pain of his body immediately ceased, and the building was calm again. Conscious of this grace, Antony regained his breath and felt free from pain. He spoke to the vision that appeared to him, saying: "Lord, where were you? Why did you not appear at the beginning in order for me not to endure such pain?" And a voice came to Antony, saying: "Antony, I was here all the time; I simply waited to witness your fight. Now, since you have endured and not yielded, I shall be your assistance forever, and I shall make your name known everywhere." Having heard this, Antony rose up and prayed, receiving such strength that he perceived he had never had more power in his body previously.[3]

If God is right there, in the middle of our struggle, then our aim is to stay there. We are to remain in the cell, to stay on the road, not to forego the journey or forget the darkness. It is all too easy for us to overlook the importance of struggle, preferring instead to secure peace and rest, or presuming to reach the stage of love prematurely. It is always easier to allow things to pass by, to go on without examination and effort. Yet, struggling means living. It is a way of fully living life and not merely observing it. It takes much time and great effort to unite the disparate, disjointed and divided parts of the self into an integrated whole. During this time and in this effort, the virtue of struggle was one of the non-negotiables in the spiritual way of the desert. The Desert Fathers and Mothers speak to us with authority, because they are in fact our fellow travelers. They never claim to have arrived; they never indicate that they have completed the journey. Remember the prayer of Arsenius:

"God, do not leave me. I have done nothing good in your sight. Rather, according to your goodness, *let me now at least make a beginning* of doing good."[4]

Second, the desert elders are also convinced that God is not only in the middle of our struggle, but that *God is always there. God is never absent,* never far away. God loves us irrespective of where we are on that journey. God loves us irrespective of who we are and what we are doing. The deepest and innermost conviction of the Desert

3. *Life of Antony,* ch. 10.
4. Arsenius 3.

Fathers and Mothers is that God loves them. That is what accounts for their joy. In spite of the difficulty and intensity of their ascetic struggle, these hermits are characterized by a sense of gladness, not of gloom.

> As he was dying, Abba Benjamin said to his disciples: "If you observe the following, you can be saved: 'Be joyful at all times! Pray without ceasing! And give thanks for all things!'"[5]

> Amma Syncletica said: "In the beginning, there are a great many struggles and a good deal of suffering for those who are advancing toward God. Afterward, however, there is ineffable joy. It is like those who wish to light a fire; at first, the smoke chokes them, and they cry. Yet by this means, they obtain what they seek, as it is said: 'Our God is a consuming fire!' (Heb. 12.24). So we, too, must kindle the divine fire in ourselves through tears and hard work."[6]

These heroes of the spirit are filled with joy; they are also characterized by humor. The desert stories are filled with witty situations and entertaining sayings. Their humor is, in my view, undoubtedly connected to their humility. If they take themselves less seriously, it is because they want to take God more seriously. They are neither obsessed by their ascetic struggle nor preoccupied with their particular virtues. The desert dwellers can be joyful because they know that they are human and that failure comes with the territory of being human. In the final analysis, or rather beyond all analysis, the desert elders are aware of one simple, yet profound truth: they know that they are not God; and they know that it is only through God that all things are possible. It may seem so obvious to us, but sometimes we forget this truth. The desert elders knew that perfection rests with the divinity; and certainly not in our frailty or in any ability that we may imagine that we have to negotiate with the divinity about our virtues and our vices.

This is why the Desert Fathers and Mothers are comfortable talking about darkness and about the struggle through darkness. They are not ashamed of their darkness or of talking about their darkest thoughts. This is also why, although their sayings at times appear crude, even harsh, to us as readers, they never in fact shame

5. Benjamin 4.
6. Syncletica 1. Abba Zosimas always speaks with a sense of humor; see *Reflections* XI, d and XII, c.

us. They are always understanding of us, always compassionate toward us. Compassion, not competition, is their goal. And so they never express any bitterness toward visitors; there is never any sense of vindictiveness. Their suggestion is not so much: "I'm OK and you're OK." On a much deeper level, it is their awareness and admission that: "I'm not OK; and you're not OK." Yet, this recognition is also their reassurance; for, they know that: "That's OK!" In truth, wherever the reality of imperfection or limitation is denied, it is God and the possibility of transcending these limitations that are rejected.

Third, and finally, there is another lesson about encountering God that may be gleaned from the teaching of these elders in the desert of early Egypt. In the struggle—in the very place where we meet God, and where we are loved by God—we too discover how to love others. It is in the struggle itself that we discern ways of embracing the weaknesses of others, and learn how to be compassionate, like God. We understand that *we are like others not primarily in our virtues and our strengths, but especially in our faults and our flaws.* In the desert, the call to perfection is received as an invitation to love; it is perceived in the light of Christ's injunction: "Be merciful, as your Father is merciful"(Luke 6.36). That is why:

> Like a god upon this earth, Abba Macarius would cover the faults of others, which he saw, as though he did not see them; and those which he heard, as though he did not hear them.[7]

> A brother, who had sinned, was turned out of the church by the priest. Abba Bessarion got up and went out with him, saying: "I too am a sinner."[8]

> One day Abba Isaac went to a monastery. He saw a brother committing a sin and condemned him. When he returned to the desert, an angel of the Lord came and stood in front of the door of his cell, and said: "I will not let you enter." But he persisted saying: "What is the matter?" The angel replied: "God has sent me to ask you where you want to throw the guilty brother whom you have condemned." Immediately, he repented and said: "I have sinned; forgive me." Then the angel said: "Get up, God has for-

7. Macarius 32.
8. Bessarion 7.

given you. But from now on, be careful not to judge someone before God has done so."[9]

Antony is no longer afraid of himself, of his sins, or indeed of God. He no longer compares himself with others. He has now learned to love. When you know and embrace your frailties, then you can learn to love yourself; then you learn to "love the Lord your God with all your heart . . . and your neighbor as yourself. There is no other commandment greater than these" (Mark 12.30-31).

> Abba Antony said: "I no longer fear God, but I love God. For love casts out fear." (John 4.18)[10]

> Abba Amoun of Nitria came to see Abba Antony and asked him: "Since my rule is stricter than yours, then how is it that your name is better known among people than mine is?" Abba Antony replied: "It is because I love God more than you do."[11]

Antony had learned that fear is an energy that restrains us; it is useful inasmuch as it assists in the discipline of abstinence. Love, on the other hand, expands us; it opens up the discipline of fasting and self-control in order to share and heal. The desert experience was a love-based theology and a love-based spirituality. Fear denies the body and the world; love affirms every detail in our life and in the world. Fear learns to let go of things; love learns to share things. The aim in the desert was precisely that: to learn to love. It was not to learn to perform impressive feats of fasting, vigil, or abstinence. Compassion, we have said, and not competition.

> Some of the elders came to visit Abba Poemen and asked him: "When we see brothers who are falling asleep during the services, should we arouse them so that they will be watchful?"

Poemen was like Antony; he too had reached the point of love. He was not anxious about not achieving some ascetic end.

> He said to them in response: "For my part, when I see a brother falling asleep, I place his head on my knees and let him rest."[12]

9. Isaac the Theban 1.
10. Antony 32.
11. Amoun of Nitria 1.
12. Poemen 92.

The unique goal was always love, not any worldly reward; indeed, not even any spiritual reward. Maybe that is why they were called "monastic," a word derived from the Greek word *monachos* (μοναχός), which implies more than merely "being alone (*monos*, μόνος)." It also signifies that they were "of a single purpose and focus." It was the same for everyone in the desert; and it should be the same for everyone in the secular world.

> A secular man of devout life came to see Abba Poemen. Now it happened that there were other brothers with the old man, asking to hear a word from him. The old man said to the faithful secular visitor: "Say a word to the brothers." When he insisted, the secular man said: "Please excuse me, abba; I myself have come here to learn." But he was still urged on by the old man. So he said: "I am a secular man. I sell vegetables and do business. I take bundles to pieces, and make smaller ones. I buy cheap and sell expensive. What is more, I do not know how to speak of the Scriptures. So I shall tell you a parable. A man said to his friends: 'I want to go and see the emperor; come with me.' The friend said to him: 'I will go with you half the way.' Then he said to another friend: 'Come and go with me to see the emperor.' The second friend replied: 'I will take you as far as the emperor's palace.' He said to a third friend: 'Come with me to the emperor.' That friend said: 'I will come and take you to the palace; and I will stay and speak in order to help you gain access to the emperor.'" The brothers asked him what was the point of the parable. He responded: "The first friend is asceticism; it leads the way. The second friend is chastity; it takes us to the gate of heaven. But the third is love; this confidently gains us access to and presents us to God our King." The brothers withdrew edified.[13]

The single-minded focus of the desert elder seeks to sharpen the focus of the divine image upon every aspect of life and upon every person in the world. In this way, all things and all people assume unique significance. The only and ultimate response to ourselves, to others and to God is love. Every other response is but a derivative dimension and secondary version of the primary reality of love.

13. Poemen 109.

# Conclusion

The desert is a profound myth. It is a powerful symbol. These fourth-century elders are reminders of fundamental truths about our world and ourselves, which we tend to forget and which they translate for all generations through the ages. They should be considered as being prophets of another reality—in many ways, the only reality—rather than strange representatives of a remote past or inaccessible examples of former times.

Nonetheless, no one can lead us into the desert. Each one of us must find our own path. Each must look for the places where we are tempted, where we are lonely, thirsty for meaning and hungry for depth. Each of us will discover the areas that need to be purified, where we can encounter God and where God speaks to us. The desert is only one expression or translation of the truth, like art, music and beauty. Each of us must discover the ways of appropriating and appreciating this truth. We may question the truth conveyed by these desert elders, though we can never deny it.

· Of course, the flight to the desert will not always be as radical as that practiced by the elders of early Christian Egypt. The ways of detachment, the moments of departure may be insignificant opportunities, ones that we may even miss if we are not attentive: a quiet moment alone; a quiet moment in the presence of a friend; a walk alone; a quiet time of camping, swimming or fishing; a time of reflection in a silent corner; a longer drive; a long wait during a short drive, when we are caught in traffic. We should enter those moments of stillness and understand them. We should also speak from those moments of silence and act out of them. We are what we do with that stillness and silence.

Opportunities present themselves to us continually, even in a busy space. We can discover the "desert," even in the noise of a city. We can all look for a place and a moment where we will struggle with our selves and encounter God. Those are the places and the moments of temptation; those are also the places and the moments of transformation. Then we shall discover the mystery of the extraordinary in the most ordinary, the wonder of the common-place, together with the surprise of beauty. When we have addressed our demons, will we not also know the presence of angels in our life?

Then we can learn, and relearn: the beauty of eating and drinking; of sleeping and waking; of walking and talking; quite simply of breathing and living. Our heart will beat in unison with the heart of the world. For then we shall know that we are less than what we are called to be when we are without one another, and that we are less than human without our world. Then we can learn new ways of caring and community. Then we can be grateful to God for "making us truly alive."

# An Introduction to Abba Zosimas:
## Reflections[1]

One of the fascinating puzzles confronting scholars dealing with this period of the fourth and fifth centuries concerns the origin and development of *The Sayings of the Desert Fathers*. How and where were the *Apophthegmata* recorded? More importantly and interestingly, how were these *Sayings* ultimately collected and published? Here a brief historical and literary excursion may be helpful in order to place the *Apophthegmata* in some cultural and spiritual context.

Already in the biography of Hilarion, written by Jerome in around 390, there is an endeavor to forge a connection between Hilarion of Palestine and Antony of Egypt. Hilarion, it seems, spent several months in the circle of Antony and his friends. This possibly occurred during the time of Antony's first emergence from the desert (around 304-305). It was Antony who inspired Hilarion to return to Palestine where his parents had died, and to give away his inheritance—albeit at the tender age of just fifteen—in order to live a life based on that of Antony. It appears that Egypt constituted a kind of model for those who aspired to a life of seclusion and silence in other, neighboring monastic regions. If Jerome is correct—for he is mostly a good story-teller—then Hilarion marks the beginning of a long and significant connection between the ways and words of the Egyptian elders and the rules and writings of their Palestinian successors. Therefore, both Epiphanius and Jerome brought back to Palestine a way of life that they clearly learned in Egypt.

Another personality from this period, Porphyry, spent some five years in Scetis of Egypt, returning in 377 to inhabit a cell in the

1. Translated from Monk Avgoustinos, *Abba Zosimas: Most Beneficial Chapters* (Jerusalem, 1913), pp. 1.25. It originally appeared in *Nea Sion* 12 (1912). The text is out of print, but a copy of it exists in the Library of St. Gregory's House, Oxford, and I am grateful to Bishop Kallistos Ware for making this available.

valley of the Jordan and, later, to become bishop of Gaza in Palestine (395-420). Indeed, *The Sayings of the Desert Fathers* include the names of other Palestinian monks, whether by origin or by adoption: Gelasius, Epiphanius, Theodore of Eleftheropolis, Hilarion, Cassian, Phocas, and Philagrios.

The connection, however, between the desert of Egypt and the dunes of Gaza became particularly noticeable when Abba Silvanus settled with his disciples in Gerara in the early fifth century. We have at our disposal twenty-six sayings, in the alphabetical collection alone, from this group of monks.

We can identify the names of four of Silvanus' disciples: Zaccharias, Mark, Netras, and Zenon. Zaccharias was perhaps the first and closest of the disciples, and also succeeded Silvanus in 414. But it is said that, "the old man loved Mark because of his obedience." He is the one who heard his elder calling him and left unfinished the letter "omega," which he was writing at the time. He was a copyist, and therefore well educated.

> It was said of Abba Silvanus that at Scetis he had a disciple called Mark, whose obedience was great. He was a scribe. . . . Once Silvanus knocked on the door of Mark's cell and said: "Mark." Hearing the old man's voice, Mark jumped up immediately and the old man sent him off to do some work. . . . Then he went into Mark's cell and picked up his book and noticed that he had begun to write the letter 'omega,' but when he had heard the old man, he had responded without finishing to write the letter.[2]

This small group was quite probably both refined and cultivated. From the *Sayings* attributed to them, we already know that they had one copyist among them. In addition to this, however, Zaccharias was learned in Hebrew, and Netras was qualified to be ordained bishop of Pharan, in the Sinai Peninsula. We also know that they liked to entertain visitors, and—at least in Sinai—they tended to a garden. In addition, the alphabetical collection tells us that Mark's mother was wealthy. These may be among the reasons that they left Egypt during the first Origenist crisis. After a brief sojourn at Sinai, they moved to Palestine, beside the river that flowed in the area of

---

2. Mark 1. See also Silvanus 1-2; Mark 1; and Netras 1. For a detailed account of the lifestyle and movements of this group, see M. Van Parys, "Abba Silvain et ses disciples," *Irénikon* 61 (1988): 315-330.

Gerara.[3] The fifth saying of Mark in the *Apophthegmata* records his wish not to accompany the group to Palestine but to remain in Sinai, where he died.

> It was said of Abba Silvanus, that when he wished to go away to Syria, his disciple Mark said to him: "Father, I do not want to leave this place [of Sinai], nor to let you go away, abba. Stay here for three days." And on the third day, Mark died.

Another well known monk and monastic author in this region was Abba Isaiah of Scetis. A later emigrant from Egypt, Isaiah had spent many years in a monastery, but had also resided in the desert of Scetis. He moved to Palestine, fleeing fame, between 431 and 451. He first settled near Eleftheropolis, moving finally to Beit Daltha near Gaza, some four miles from Thavatha. There he stayed for several decades, serving for his contemporaries and visitors as a living example of the old Scetiote ascetic life, until his death in 489.[4]

This is not the last that we hear of these places. For, Gaza and its environs are indelibly marked by the presence of two remarkable elders in the next century: Barsanuphius and John; and by the products of their teaching: their *Letters: Questions and Answers,* as well as by their disciples, especially Dorotheus. Indeed, the city of Thavatha is mentioned on the Madeba Map, a mosaic map from a church in Madeba (modern Jordan) dating from the latter part of Justinian's era[5] and thus almost coinciding with the latter part of the lives of Barsanuphius and John.

---

3. Silvanus, Saying suppl. 1, in J.-Cl. Guy, *Researches sur le tradition grecque des Apophthegmata Patrum,* 2nd ed. (Brussels, 1984), p. 47. While *The Sayings of the Desert Fathers* provide much material for someone hoping to reconstruct the daily routine and the general development of the group around Silvanus, Sozomen offers the clearest historical evidence outside of the monastic milieu. See his *Historia Ecclesiastica* VI, 32, 8 in J. Bidez and G.C. Hansen, eds., *Die Griechischen Christlichen Schriftsteller der Ersten Jahrhunderte* 50 (Berlin, 1960), pp. 288-289.

4. More on Abba Isaiah in J. Chryssavgis and P.R. Penkett, *Abba Isaiah of Scetis: Ascetic Discourses* (Kalamazoo MI: Cistercian Publications, 2002).

5. See C.A.M. Glucker, *The City of Gaza in the Roman and Byzantine Periods,* BAR International Series 325 (Oxford, 1987), pp. 18-20; and M. Avi-Yonah, *The Madeba Mosaic Map* (Jerusalem, 1954), pp. 16-18. On the letters of the two elders, see F. Neyt and P. de Angelis, *Barsanuphe et Jean de Gaza, Correspondance* vol. I, i in *Sources chrétiennes* 426 (Paris, 1997). More on Barsanuphius and John in the translation of and introduction to their correspondence by J. Chryssavgis [forthcoming: Cistercian Publications].

We do not know exactly when Barsanuphius, himself an Egyptian monk, entered the region of Thavatha and chose to be enclosed as a recluse in a nearby cell. From this position, he offered counsel to a number of ascetics who were gradually attracted around the Old Man as he developed a reputation for discernment and compassion. One of these monks, Abba Seridos, who also attended to Barsanuphius, was appointed abbot of a monastic community, probably established in order to organize the increasing number of monks that looked to Barsanuphius as their elder. Seridos was the only person permitted to communicate with Barsanuphius, acting as a mediator for those who wished to submit questions in writing and to receive a response through the same avenue.

Some time between 525 and 527, another hermit, named John, came to live beside Barsanuphius, who surrendered his own cell to him, while he moved to a new cell nearby. Barsanuphius became known as "the holy Old Man" or "the Great Old Man," a Coptic term familiar among Egyptian circles, and ascribed also by Palladius to Antony "the Great." John is simply called "the Other Old Man." The two shared the same way of life and supported one another's ministry.

There are around eight hundred and fifty letters that survive from these two Old Men, a treasure house of information from a variety of people about life at the time. Monks in communities, hermits in isolation, spouses in families, professionals in society: all asking questions, submitted in writing to the wise elder, and receiving a response through their scribes. The responses of the elders are spontaneous and balanced, wise and witty, reminiscent of their predecessors in the desert of Egypt.

The lifestyles of the ascetics living in Egypt and later in Palestine—or, indeed, their ascetic ways of dying unto themselves and the world—were not the only aspects that were imitated and copied during this period. In particular, it was the *Apophthegmata Patrum* that permeated throughout the Christian world and were preserved by the disciples of these same sages, and the disciples of their disciples. Thence, they were transferred into the whole of the ancient world and translated into all languages of early Christendom. One of the most likely places that these *Sayings* were recollected and then collected was in Palestine, partly due to its geographical proximity to Egypt, but also due to the steady progression of Egyptian monks to the southern parts of Judaea. This diffusion of the *Apophthegmata* on the one hand, and the emigration of the Fathers and Mothers on the other, is surely not unrelated. Already, Fr. Lucien Regnault has demonstrated how *The Sayings of the Desert Fathers*, in both their alphabetical and anonymous or systematic collections, are found in seminal texts of the time. Such texts include the *Life of Saint Melanie the Younger*, attributed to her confidant and chaplain Gerontius and dating to the middle of the fifth century; the *Life of Saint Euthymius*, written by Cyril of Scythopolis in the latter half of the sixth century; and the *Reflections* of Zosimas, who founded a community in the first half of the sixth century. In particular, Regnault highlights the role of the monasteries of Seridos and of Dorotheus in the Gaza region, and the *Correspondence* of Barsanuphius and John as well as the *Works* of their disciple Dorotheus, all of which offer the richest documentation in this regard.[6]

Melanie's *Life* refers to one of the sayings of the *Apophthegmata*; Euthymius' *Life* contains three such sayings; while Zosimas' treatise makes numerous citations of these sayings, implying perhaps that the latter borrowed these from existing written texts. Euthymius and Zosimas also reveal having heard various sayings of the *Apophthegmata* from others, which attests to the fact that these were widely known and, possibly, even accessible more or less everywhere in monastic circles of lower Palestine by the middle of the sixth century. Indeed, Zosimas' reference to "the sayings of the holy elders"[7] is perhaps the earliest such characterization of the sayings with this specific title.

The *Reflections* of Abba Zosimas appear for the first time in English translation below. We are told by the author that:

> The blessed Zosimas always loved to read these *Sayings* all the time; they were almost like the air that he breathed.[8]

6. L. Regnault, "Les *Apophtegmes des Pères* en Palestine aux Ve et Ve siècles," *Irénikon* 54 (1981): 320-330.

7. Cf. *Reflections*, ch. 12 (Avgoustinos edition, Jerusalem, 1913), p. 17. Also found in John Moschus, *Spiritual Meadow*, ch. 212, pp. 190-191 (PG 87: 3104-3105).

8. See *Reflections* [below] XII, b.

Like *The Sayings of the Desert Fathers* themselves, these "reflections" were spoken and not written down by Zosimas. In content and style, they very much resemble the *Ascetic Discourses* of Abba Isaiah of Scetis. Zosimas flourished between 475 and 525, from the period just after the fourth Ecumenical Council (in 451) until around the time of the great Gaza elders, Barsanuphius, John and Dorotheus.[9] He is mentioned several times by Dorotheus of Gaza, who knew him personally and visited him as his younger contemporary and compatriot. Dorotheus may in fact be the compiler of the *Reflections* of Abba Zosimas.

The *Letters* of Barsanuphius and John, again dating to the first half of the sixth century, frequently quote or evoke the *Sayings*. In fact, there are at least eighty direct references to the *Apophthegmata* themselves, while numerous phrases recommend them as a basis for spiritual practice and progress, sometimes by name (sixteen times) but mostly by implication (thirty-four times). There are at least fifty-five references to *The Sayings of the Desert Fathers* in the writings of Dorotheus alone. He also seems to be the first writer to designate the *Apophthegmata* as the "*Gerontikon*" (or, the *Book of Elders*).[10] Might, therefore, this Dorotheus also be one of those responsible for the collection of the *Sayings* themselves? Certainly Dorotheus is the only ancient witness to the single saying attributed to Basil in the alphabetical collection of *The Sayings of the Desert Fathers*,[11] while both Barsanuphius and Dorotheus refer to the *Rules* of Saint Basil.

During the fourth and the early fifth centuries, the golden age during which *The Sayings of the Desert Fathers* flourished, the words of the elders were preserved both in the heart and by word of mouth. They were precisely that: sayings; and these circulated both in Egypt and in Palestine as a result of the fluid movement between the two "seminal" lands, but especially as a result of the eastward influx of

---

9. Zosimas mentions a visit to the monastery of St. Gerasimus, which was founded after 451, while Evagrius Scholasticus mentions in his *Ecclesiastical History* IV, 7 (PG 86: 2713-2717) that Zosimas predicted an earthquake that occurred in 525.

10. See his *Teachings* I, 13 (PG 88: 1633C) in *Sources chrétiennes* 92 (Paris, 1952). G.W.H. Lampe's *Patristic Lexikon* (Oxford, 1991), p. 313 refers to a letter by Nilus; however, this is not authentic.

11. See L. Regnault, "Les *Apophtegmes des Pères*," p. 328; and Dorotheus, *Teachings* 24 in *Sources chrétiennes* 92, pp. 182-184.

monks from Egypt to Palestine, whether forcefully or freely. It seems that later generations of ascetic leaders and authors sensed the importance of transmitting, even translating, their Egyptian roots for future generations in both East and West. Thus, Evagrius and John Cassian included several sayings from the *Apophthegmata* in their influential writings.[12] Abba Isaiah of Scetis inserted numerous of these sayings, both recognizable and original, in his *Ascetic Discourses*, possibly regarding himself as responsible for preserving and promoting the words of the elders that he knew and lived with in Egypt. The abundant references to the *Sayings* in the *Letters* of Barsanuphius and John further attest to their concern that the ways and words of the ancient elders be pondered and practiced.

Indeed, the *Letters* of Barsanuphius and John, and especially the ones addressed by, and to, Dorotheus of Gaza (*Letters* 252-338), reveal yet another element that gradually disappeared from *The Sayings of the Desert Fathers*, as these began to be collated and edited. For, the original transmission of the wisdom of the Egyptian desert preserved the spontaneity of the profound advice and impressive actions of the Desert Fathers and Mothers. However, during the stage of transition from an oral culture to a written text, the *Sayings* became a little more static and began to lose sight of the personal element that sparked these words; more particularly and significantly, the process and struggle that shaped these words was also concealed. What was recorded was the intense drop of wisdom, without the stages that led to the final product. What is missing is the ongoing process—all of the contentions, hesitations, and limitations of the spiritual aspirant. *The Sayings of the Desert Fathers*, for instance, often present the spiritual reality in *the way that it should be, rather than in the way that it is*—with all the denials, the doubts, and the temptations. Yet, in Barsanuphius and John, we witness each of the painful stages unfolding in slow motion before our very eyes, like a film consisting of many gradually changing pictures. Here is one example of this progressive development of a thought and response.

> Question 293. Question from the same brother to the same Old Man: If a brother does something that is not very significant, yet I

---

12. Evagrius toward the end of the *Praktikos* and in chapters 106-112 of his treatise *On Prayer* (PG 79: 1189-1192). And Cassian in his *Institutes* V, 24-41.

am afflicted by this act on account of my own will, what should I do? Should I keep silent and not give rest to my heart, or should I speak to him with love and not remain troubled? And if the matter afflicts others, and not me, should I speak for the sake of the others? Or would this appear as if I have just taken on a cause?

Response by John. If it is a matter that is not sinful but insignificant, and you speak simply in order to give rest to your heart, then it is to your defeat. For, you were not able to endure it as a result of your weakness. Just blame yourself and be silent. However, if the matter afflicts others, tell your abbot; and whether he speaks or tells you to speak, you will be carefree.

Question 294. Question from the same person to the same Old Man: If I speak to the abbot for the sake of the others, I suspect that the brother will be troubled; so what should I do? And if he afflicts both the others and me, should I speak for the sake of the others, or should I keep silent in order not to satisfy myself? If I suspect that he will not be grieved, should I also speak for myself, or should I force myself against this?

Response by John. As far as the turmoil of the brother is concerned, if you speak to the abbot, then you have nothing to worry about. When it is necessary to speak for the sake of others, and you are worried about it, then speak for them. As for yourself, only force yourself not to speak.

Question 295. Question from the same to the same: But my thought tells me that if my brother is troubled against me, he will become my enemy, thinking that I slandered him to the abbot.

Response by John. This thought of yours is wicked; for, it wants to prevent you from correcting your brother. Therefore, do not prevent yourself from speaking, but do so according to God. For indeed, the sick that are being healed will even speak against their doctors; yet the latter do not care, knowing that the same shall thank them afterward.

Question 296. Question from the same to the same Old Man: If I look at my thought and notice that it is not for the brother's benefit that I wish to speak to the abbot, but with the purpose of slandering him, should I speak or keep silent?

Response by John. Advise your thought to speak according to God and not for the sake of slander. And if your thought is conquered by criticism, even so speak to your abbot and confess to him your criticism, so that both of you may be healed—the one who was at fault and the one who was critical.

Question 297. Question from the same to the same: If my thought does not allow me to confess to the abbot that I am speaking to him with the purpose of slandering the brother, what should I do? Should I speak or not?

Response. Do not say anything to him, and the Lord will take care of the matter. For, it is not necessary for you to speak when this harms your soul. God will take care of the brother's correction as He wills.

There is a further reason why the collector and editor of the *Apophthegmata* may be from the circle of monks in Seridos' community. A schematic comparison between the Egyptian and Palestinian elders may be helpful in this regard. Isaiah, Zosimas, Barsanuphius and Dorotheus all seem to *display certain characteristics in common with and in contrast to the desert dwellers*. For instance, each of these four prominent figures is balanced and un-polemical in their nature and in their counsel, much like the disposition of the Egyptian monastics whose sayings are preserved in the collections. In general, they do not reveal the confessional rifts that affected so much of Christendom during this period. They are far less militant than other representatives of both the Chalcedonian and non-Chalcedonian circles. Other contemporary ascetics, such as Sabas, while compassionate and non-judgmental in their outlook, are nevertheless deliberately and defensively concerned with confessional doctrine. It is no wonder, then, that an icon of the Great Old Man graces the altar-cloth fresco in the Great Church of Wisdom in Constantinople, beside those of Antony of Egypt and Ephraim the Syrian.

Yet, the Gaza elders also differ from their Egyptian counterparts inasmuch as they are on the whole more educated and widely read. This feature may not be entirely unknown among the Desert Fathers and Mothers, but it is rather exceptional. Barsanuphius' responses to questions about Origenist tendencies among certain representatives of the monastic tradition (in *Letters* 600-607), together with John's explanations of the Great Old Man's words, reveal an elder who appreciates fine intellectual distinctions without at the same time being absorbed by these to the detriment of his life of prayer. Thus, in another set of thirteen questions (between *Letters* 151 and 167), being responses to a certain Euthymius whose mind is almost obsessed with allegorical interpretations and details, Barsanuphius recommends humility and silence.

At some point in time, then, between the work of Abba Isaiah of Scetis and the correspondence of the two Old Men of Gaza, there appears to have occurred a shift in the appreciation of the *Sayings*. Abba Isaiah senses that he is a *part of the tradition of the Desert Fathers*, that he has transplanted this tradition from the chosen land to an adopted land, and that he is obliged to keep that memory alive in his new homeland. Abba Barsanuphius and his disciples, particularly the gifted Dorotheus, sense that they are a *part of a new tradition*, closely linked to the past and yet at the same time clearly looking to a different experience and a different environment. The attitude of Abba Isaiah and Abba Zosimas is backward-looking to the golden age of Egypt. Barsanuphius and Dorotheus are forward-looking to the diverse monastic population that they are serving and the different monastic culture that they are confronted with. In fact, their presence in the region of Gaza, that intersection and cross-section of peoples and pilgrims, may well be the reason why the alphabetical collection of *The Sayings of the Desert Fathers* bring together so many pieces from the worlds of Egypt, Sinai, Palestine, Asia Minor, Syria, and as far east as Persia. The region also numbered Arabs, Greeks, Latins, Armenians, Georgians, and others. Moreover, the monks of this region were deeply influenced by Barsanuphius' openness toward foreigners imposed by a dynamic of positive interaction. Indeed, Barsanuphius was quite clear about the role of his contemporaries; it was, as he determines in *Letter* 569, to pray for the salvation of the whole world, orthodox and non-orthodox, pious and pagan:

> There are three men, perfect in God, who have exceeded the measure of humanity and received the authority to loose and bind, to forgive and hold sins. These stand before the shattered world, keeping the whole world from complete and sudden annihilation. Through their prayers, God combines His chastisement with His mercy. And it has been told to them, that God's wrath will last a little longer. Therefore, pray with them. For the prayers of these three are joined at the entrance to the spiritual altar of the Father of lights. They share in each other's joy and gladness in heaven.

And when they turn once again toward the earth, they share in each other's mourning and weeping for the evils that occur and attract His wrath. These three are John in Rome and Elias in Corinth, and another in the region of Jerusalem. I believe that they will achieve His great mercy. Yes, they will indeed achieve it. Amen.

Undoubtedly, Barsanuphius possessed the discerning boldness before God, as well as the humanity to claim within his heart that he was the third of these ascetics.

In brief, Abba Isaiah and Abba Zosimas lamented over the loss of the past, while Barsanuphius and Dorotheus learned ways of relating to the present and looking to the future. The song of Isaiah and Zosimas declared with sorrow: "By the rivers of Babylon, there we sat down and there we wept, when we remembered Zion" (Psalm 137.1); the challenge of Barsanuphius and Dorotheus discerned: "How could we sing the Lord's song in a foreign land?" (Psalm 137.4) They understood that the tradition of the *Apophthegmata* demanded more than just repetition; it required unpacking and appropriation in a new way.

# The Text of the
# Reflections (Διαλογισμοί)
# of Abba Zosimas

## I. On Detachment

a.    When he began, the blessed Abba Zosimas spoke in the following manner. First, he would perform the sign of the cross over his mouth. He would say that, when the divine Word became human, He granted abundant grace to those who believed and who still believe in Him. For, it is possible to believe even now, indeed even to begin from this day, if we so desire. After all, our desire depends on our free will, with the cooperation also of grace. Thus, it is possible for whoever so desires, to regard the whole world as being nothing.

b.    Moreover, he would take whatever he could find—whether a nail or some thread, or anything else of insignificant value—and say: "Who would ever fight or argue over this; or else, who would keep a grudge or be afflicted over this? Unless it be someone who has truly lost his mind. Therefore, a person of God, who is progressing and advancing, should consider the whole world as this nail, even if that person actually possesses the entire world. For, as I always like to say: 'It is not possessing something that is harmful, but being attached to it.'"

c.    Who is ignorant of the fact that the human body is more precious than anything else that we may have? Then, how is it that, when circumstances demand, we are ordered to despise it (Matt. 18.8)? If this is what happens with the body, how much more so does it apply to external matters? Just as it is not appropriate to disregard material things unnecessarily, for no reason at all, it is also not proper to throw oneself before death. For, this would be foolishness. Rather, we are called to await the appropriate time, in order that we may be prepared.

d.    He remembered the brother who owned some vegetables,[1] and used to say: "Did he not sow the seed, or toil in labor, or plant and nurture their growth? Did he perhaps uproot them or throw them away? No. Yet, he possessed these vegetables as if he did not in fact own them (1 Cor. 7.30-31). He was not therefore worried when his elder, wishing to test him, began to destroy them. This appeared as nothing to him; instead, he concealed his feelings. Moreover, when one root remained, he said to his elder: 'Father, if you wish, you may leave it, so that we may share a meal.' Then, that holy elder understood that his disciple was genuinely a servant of God and not of the vegetables. So he told him: 'The Spirit of God has found rest upon you, brother.' Now, if the brother had been attached to the vegetables, this would immediately have become apparent, because he would have been afflicted and troubled. Instead, he showed that he possessed them without actually owning them."

e.    Abba Zosimas also used to say that the demons pay attention to these matters. In addition, if they notice someone not being attached to things, because they are neither afflicted nor troubled by them, then they know that such a person may walk on this earth but does not in fact have an earthly mentality.

## II. i. On Enduring Insults

a.    Again, he used to say: "There are different levels in people's desires. One person may desire something fervently, and that desire will be capable of leading that person to God at one moment; whereas another person will not reach that point in fifty years on account of a lukewarm desire."

b.    When the demons notice that someone has been insulted or shamed or harmed or suffered something of the like, and yet that person is sorry not so much for what has happened but for not being able to endure these courageously, then the demons are afraid of such a strong will. For, they know that this person has

---

1. See *Apophthegmata*, Nau no. 343.

touched upon the way of truth and has decided to walk in accordance with the commandments of God.

## ii. The Prayer of Pachomius

a.    Abba Zosimas would remember Saint Pachomius, whose elder brother cried out, saying: "Stop being vainglorious!" This was because Pachomius wanted to expand the monastery as a result of the divine vision that he was granted.[2] Moreover, as it says, he felt moved to anger, and justifiably so; yet, still he did not say anything in response. Instead, remaining in control of his heart, on the following night, he descended into a small basement, and began to weep, praying thus: "God, the fleshly mentality still remains in me, and I still live according to the flesh. Woe is me! For, I shall lose my life, as it is written (Rom. 8.12-13). Even after so much ascetic discipline and spiritual preparation, I am still moved to anger; even if it is with good reason. Have mercy on me, Lord, in order that I may not perish. If the enemy finds even the slightest part in me, unless you support me, I shall submit to him. For, 'if someone keeps your whole law, but fails in one point, then that person has become accountable for all of it' (James 2.10). In addition, I believe that, if your abundant mercies assist me, I shall henceforth learn how to walk in the way of your saints, moving forward to those things, which lie before me (Phil. 3.13). For, they appropriately put the enemy to shame. How shall I be able, Lord, to teach those whom you have called with me to choose this way of life, when I have not first conquered the enemy myself?" Having prayed in this manner, he remained there the whole night long, repeating the same words and weeping, until the next morning dawned. Indeed, from his sweat, the soles of his feet became like clay. For, it was summer and the place was extremely hot.

b.    And the blessed Abba Zosimas said in astonishment: "Were not Pachomius' tears without limit (Psalm 79.6)? How could God not grant His gifts to such a will? As for me, I am convinced that, during that night, God granted to Pachomius everything for which he had asked, namely to be dead unto all things."

---

2. See the *Life of Pachomius*, ch. 15.

## III. Healing from Christ

a.　　He also said: "If someone perceives that another person has brought affliction or harm or slander or any other evil, and in return the same one weaves thoughts against that other person, then one is actually conspiring against one's own soul, just as if the demons were doing this. One is actually able to bring this upon oneself. What do I mean by 'weaving'? If one does not imagine the other person to be like a healer, then one is bringing upon oneself the greatest harm. Why do you say that the other person has caused you suffering? That person has actually brought you cleansing. Moreover, you should think of that person as a healer, sent to you by Christ. You ought to suffer for the sake of that person (Acts 9.16), and you should regard that person as your benefactor."

b.　　If you have not been alienated from evil, and do not wish to be alienated from it, then the Lord your God is not to blame for this. The act of suffering is quite appropriate for a soul that is unhealthy. Were you not unhealthy, you would not be suffering. Therefore, you owe your brother a favor; because it is through him that you have come to know your illness. You should accept whatever he offers you, as if it were healing medicine sent to you by Jesus. Yet, not only do you not express gratitude to him, but you even weave thoughts against your brother. What you are really saying to Jesus is that you do not wish to be healed by Him; you do not wish to receive His medicine; you prefer to decay in your wounds; and you wish to submit to the demons. What, then, can the Lord do? For, inasmuch as the Lord is good, He gave us His holy commandments in order to purge our evils, by cauterizing and cleansing them. Therefore, anyone who wishes and longs to be healed is obliged to endure whatever the doctor offers in order to be delivered from the illness. Indeed, no patient is happy being amputated or cauterized or cleansed with enema. Rather, every patient thinks about such things with disgust. Nonetheless, that same patient is convinced that it is impossible to be healed of one's illness without these. One surrenders, then, to the doctor, knowing that, in return for a small amount of disgust, a great deal of healing will result for an unhealthy condition and chronic illness.

c.　　Someone that brings you harm represents the burning medicine of Jesus. If you endure that harm willingly, then you are healed of your greed; if you cannot endure it, then you are bringing harm to yourself. Do not blame your brother. Unfortunately, we are tempted to forget to blame ourselves, and instead of welcoming the medicine of Christ, we start weaving thoughts against those who are our benefactors, as if we were out of our minds.

## IV. On Temptation and Humiliation

a.     He used to say: "'Take away the thoughts, and no one can become holy.[3] One who avoids a beneficial temptation is avoiding eternal life.' One of the saints said: 'Who procured those crowns for the holy martyrs, except their persecutors? Who granted such great glory to Saint Stephen, but they who stoned him?'" In addition, he always used to quote the passage from Evagrius: "'I do not blame those who accuse me, but rather I call them my benefactors.'[4] More-over: 'I do not despise the spiritual doctor, who brings the medicine of dishonor to the vainglorious soul. My fear is that it may be said about my soul, that: "We have healed Babylon, but it has not been healed"(Jer. 28.9).'"[5]

b.     He also said: "Evagrius feared that he might be accused by Christ, who might tell him: 'Evagrius, you were ill from vainglory, and I administered unto you the medicine of dishonor in order that you might be healed. Yet you were not healed.' We should also know that no one tells us the truth so much as those people who blame us."

c.     Abba Zosimas used to say: "The Lord knows, as 'the one who tests hearts and minds' (Psalm 7.10), that, even if everyone praises and exalts everything that I do, nevertheless this deserves blame, shame and scorn. If someone were to tell me: 'You did such and such well,' I would respond: 'What good can I do?' No one lies so much as those people who praise and exalt me; and no one tells the truth so much as they who accuse and humiliate me, as I have already said. In fact, even they are not saying the entire truth. For they have only been able to see but a tiny part of the ocean of our wrongdoing. Otherwise, they would have completely repudiated

3. *Sayings*, Antony 4-5.
4. Evagrius, *Letter* 52, ed. Frankenberg, pp. 600-601.
5. *Ibid.*, *Letter* 51, pp. 598-599.

our soul, turning away from it as if from defilement, stench and some unclean spirit. Indeed, even if people could be transformed into words in order to insult us, I am certain that no one would be properly able to describe our dishonor. For, everyone that insults and blames only expresses a part and not the whole of what we are. If the righteous Job said: 'I am full of shame' (Job 10.15)—and there is nothing more to add to that 'fullness'—then what would we say, when we are like an ocean of every evil? The devil has humiliated us with every sin; and we should be grateful for this humiliation. For, those who are grateful for their humiliation crush the devil. As the holy Fathers have said: 'When humility is lowered to the depths of Hades, then it is raised up to Heaven. And if pride is raised up to Heaven, then it is lowered to the depths of Hades.'"[6]

d.    He also said: "Who could ever persuade a humble person to weave thoughts against someone else? For, no matter what a humble person suffers or hears, that person will see this as an opportunity to insult and shame himself."

e.    In addition, he used to recall how the priests once cast Abba Moses outside of the altar, saying: "Get out, you Ethiopian." Abba Moses began to rebuke himself, saying: "Your skin is as black as ashes. You are not a man, so why should you be allowed to be among other men?"[7]

## V. i. The Way of the Saints

a.    He also used to say: "Whatever may happen to a humble person, that person turns toward prayer and considers everyone as a benefactor. However, we have deviated from the way of truth and the directions of the saints. Instead, we seek to forge our own way, according to our wicked desires. Nevertheless, what can be easier than to listen to that holy and practical teacher, Abba Ammonas, who says: 'Pay close attention to yourself. Then, if someone should afflict you in any matter whatsoever, you will be silent. You will not say anything at all until your heart is softened through unceasing prayer. Afterward, you are able to console your brother.'"[8]

6. *Apophthegmata*, Nau no. 381.
7. *Sayings*, Moses 3-4.
8. Cf. *Patrologia Orientalis*, vol. 11, p. 466. See also Abba Isaiah, *Ascetic Discourses* 27.

b.    For, a person that longs for the true and straight way will rebuke himself harshly when troubled by something like this. That person will always practice self-examination, saying: "My soul, why have you lost your mind? Why are you troubled like those who are insane? It is precisely this, which indicates how unwell in fact you are. Had you been healthy, you would not have been troubled. Why do you neglect to blame yourself and begin accusing your brother for revealing to you your illness both in deed and in truth? Learn the commandments of Christ: 'When He was abused, He did not return abuse; when He suffered, He did not threaten' (1 Pet. 2.23). Listen to Him, when He says and when He shows us in reality: 'I gave my back to those who struck me, and my cheeks to those who beat me. I did not hide my face from insult and spitting' (Is. 50.6). Yet, you, wretched soul, just because of a single insult and dishonor, sit there and weave thousands of thoughts, ultimately conspiring against your own soul in the manner of the demons. After all, what more can a demon do to such a soul, that it has not already done to itself? We see the cross of Christ, we read of His passion each day, what He suffered for us. Yet, we cannot endure the slightest insult. We have indeed deviated from the straight way."

c.    He also said: "Even if one were to live as long as Mathusala, and yet not travel this straight way, which all of the saints have journeyed, namely the way of courageously enduring dishonor and harm, then such a person will advance neither a lot nor a little, but will simply end up wasting all of those years."

### ii. Amma Dionysia

a.    Again he said: "When I was once with the blessed Dionysia, a brother asked her for some alms; and she gave him whatever she could. However, since he received less than he had asked for, he began to insult her, speaking improperly about her and about me. When she heard this, she was hurt and sought to harm him. Therefore, on learning this, I told her: 'What are you doing, conspiring against yourself? You are removing every virtue from your soul. For, what is it that you worthily endure, by comparison with those things, which Christ endured for you? I know, my lady, that you have distributed all your possessions as if they were worthless. Nevertheless, unless you acquire meekness, then you will be like a forger beating an iron nugget but producing no vessel.'" He also told her: "Saint

Ignatius the God-bearer says: 'I require meekness, through which all of the power of the prince of this age is abolished.'[9] The sign of abolishing this world is not being troubled when someone insults you."

b.    There are times when a person will ignore large sums of money; nevertheless, when it comes to a small needle, one's attachment to it may cause one much trouble. Then, the small needle replaces the large amount of money. Therefore, one becomes a slave of the needle, or the monastic cap, or the handkerchief, or the book, instead of being a servant of God.

c.    It was well said once by a wise person, that the soul has as many masters as it has passions. And again, the Apostle says: "People are slaves to whatever masters them" (2 Pet. 2.19).

d.    Upon hearing these words, Amma Dionysia was attentive and amazed. She replied: "You will surely find the God for whom you long." Then, the blessed Zosimas added: "The soul desires salvation. Yet, in also desiring after and being preoccupied with vain matters, it seeks to avoid pain. Yet, truly, it is not the commandments that are burdensome (1 John 5.3), but only our evil desires. For, we have become accustomed to despise everything, whether for fear of the sea or else for fear of thieves. Therefore, we readily surrender, even if we know that we shall die after a few years. Nevertheless, even if only for the sake of living a little while longer, we are prepared to despise everything. Indeed, we consider ourselves fortunate if we lose everything, but still save our lives from those thieves or from the sea. And, whereas prior to this, someone might have been obsessed about acquiring a small amount of money, now that same person eagerly overlooks everything for the sake of gaining even a little more of this temporary life. Why, then, do we not think in the same way about eternal life? Why is the fear of God, as one saint put it, not as valid as our fear of the sea?"

In order to illustrate this, the blessed Zosimas related the following story, which he had heard from others.

9. *Letter to the Trallians* IV, 2.

## VI. The Story of the Stone-Carver

a.     "Once upon a time, a stone-carver,[10] whom they also call a gem-engraver because he possessed certain precious stones and diamonds, embarked on a ship together with his sons, in order to travel for purposes of trade. It so happened that he providentially grew to admire one of the servants on the boat, who would attend to him, and the two shared meals together. One day, this particular servant overheard the sailors whispering and planning among themselves to throw the stone-carver overboard because of the precious stones that he possessed. So the servant, who was deeply saddened, came to the stone-carver in order to attend to him, as it was his custom. The latter asked him why he was sad that day, but the servant kept this to himself and did not respond at all. Therefore, the stone-carver asked him again: 'Please tell me, what is the matter with you?' Then, the servant broke down in tears and told him: 'The sailors are conspiring against you in such and such a way.' The stone-carver said: 'Is this true?' The servant replied: 'Yes. That is what they have planned among themselves.' Then, the stone-carver called his sons and told them: 'Whatever I tell you, do it without hesitation.' Then, he spread out a sheet and began to say to them: 'Bring me the treasure boxes'; and they did. The stone-carver began to lay out all of the gemstones. After spreading them out on the sheet, he began to say: 'Is this what life is about? Am I to risk battling for my life in the seas for the sake of these? Am I about to die in a short while, without taking with me anything from this world?' And he said to his sons: 'Empty everything into the sea.' On hearing his words, they cast everything into the sea. The sailors were astonished, but their conspiracy was abolished."

b.     Moreover, the blessed Zosimas said: "Let us consider how, as soon as this thought occurred to him, that stone-carver became a philosopher in both his actions and his words. And all this, simply in order to gain a little more of this life. He was of course right in doing so. For, he thought to himself: 'If I am to die, then what do I have to gain from these precious stones?' Yet, we are unable to endure even a little harm for the sake of Christ's commandments. If it is necessary to grieve at all, then we should grieve for the loss of

10. John Moschus, *Spiritual Meadow*, ch. 203 (PG 87: 3096).

that person who has harmed us, not for the loss of our possessions. For, that person has done injustice to himself by being cast out of the heavenly kingdom. 'Wrongdoers shall not inherit the kingdom of God' (1 Cor. 6.9). As for you that have been done injustice, the person that has wronged you has in fact procured life for you. It is indeed said: 'Rejoice and be glad, for your reward is great in Heaven' (Matt. 5.12). Yet, instead of grieving over the loss of one of Christ's members, we sit and weave thoughts about corruptible and insignificant matters, which are easily lost and worth nothing. We are truly and rightly condemning ourselves."

c.     In effect, God has placed us in an order of many members, which have Christ our God as their head, as the Apostle said: "Just as the body is one and has many members, and the head of all is Christ" (1 Cor. 12.12). Therefore, when your brother afflicts you, he is hurting you like a hand or an eye that suffers from some illness. Yet, even when we are in pain, we do not cut off our hand and throw it away; nor do we pull out our eye, but consider the rejection of each of these as being a very serious matter. Instead, we place on these members the sign of Christ, which is more precious than anything else, entreating the saints to pray for them, as well as offering our own fervent prayers to God on their behalf. In addition to this, we apply medication and plaster in order to heal the sore member.[11] Therefore, in the same way that you pray for your eye or your hand to heal and no longer to hurt, you should also do that for your brother. Nevertheless, when we see the members of Christ hurting in this way, not only do we not grieve for them, but we even curse them. Truly, such conduct is appropriate for someone without any compassion.

d.     He also used to say: "A person who has acquired a compassionate heart or a sympathetic love first brings joy and benefit to himself, and then also to his neighbor. On the other hand, the converse also holds true; evil consumes and annihilates the person who possesses it. Such a person imagines doing harm to his neighbor, whether in matters of money or glory, or even bodily harm, although in so doing such a person is actually depriving himself of

11. Abba Dorotheus, *Instruction* VI, 77.

life." He also used to quote the saying: "'One who does not harm the soul does not harm any person.'"[12]

## VII. The Secret of Peace

a.    The blessed Abba Zosimas also used to say: "Once someone said to me: 'Abba, the commandments are numerous and the intellect is darkened when it considers which ones to keep and which ones not to keep.' I responded: 'This should not trouble you. Rather, consider the following. When you are unattached to things, then you easily acquire virtue. And when you do not seek after things, you will not be mindful of wrong done to you.'"

b.    How much labor does it require to pray for one's enemies? Do you need to plow the earth? Do you have to embark on a journey? Does it cost you any money? If you are grateful when you are dishonored, then you have already become a disciple of the holy Apostles, who would go on their way rejoicing that they were being put to shame for the name of Christ (Acts 5.41). Indeed, they endured this, while they were clean and holy, simply for the name of Christ; whereas we deserve to be dishonored on account of our sins. In fact, we are dishonored, even if no one shames and curses us: "You rebuke the insolent, accursed ones, who wander from your commandments" (Psalm 119.21). It is not appropriate for everyone to be dishonored for the name of Christ; this belongs to the holy and pure ones, as I said before. As for us, however, it is appropriate to accept and confess with thanksgiving that we are rightly dishonored on account of our evil deeds.

c.    Nevertheless, our wretched soul, while being aware of its impure actions, and understanding that it deservedly suffers whatever it suffers, sits back and falsely reasons with its own conscience, weaving thoughts and saying: "Such and such spoke against me, and shamed me, and insulted me." In this way, the soul is conspiring against itself and substituting the demons. What we see happening in the crafts also happens in the art of the soul. For, a master conveys a particular craft to a disciple and then allows the disciple to work on his own, no longer regarding it as necessary to sit beside

12. Unidentified saying.

the disciple but only on occasion paying a visit in order to see whether the disciple has neglected the craft or perhaps even lost it. In the same way, the demons that see the soul obeying and readily accepting evil thoughts surrender the soul to the demonic craft. They do not need to sit beside it all the time, knowing that the soul is sufficiently capable of conspiring against itself; they simply visit the soul from time to time in order to see whether it has neglected their craft.

d. What can be simpler than to love everyone and be loved by everyone? What great comfort do we not receive from the commandments of Christ? Nonetheless, our free will is not passionate enough.[13] If it were truly passionate, then by the grace of God everything would appear simple for our free will. As I have frequently told you, a small inclination of our desire is able to attract God for our assistance. Moreover, as the sacred Antony says: "Virtue only requires our desire." Or again: "We do not need to make a great journey in order to reach the heavenly kingdom, nor do we need to cross the seas in order to acquire virtue."[14] What rest is lacking from the meek and humble person? Truly: "The meek shall inherit the land, and delight themselves in abundant prosperity" (Psalm 37.11).

## VIII. Lessons on Humility

a. Again, the blessed Abba Zosimas used to say: "Once, a brother and I were traveling together with some lay people on the way to Neapolis, and we arrived at a place where there was a customs house. The lay people were familiar with the custom and paid their due. The brother who was with me started to object, saying: 'How dare you demand money from monks?' When I heard this, I told him: 'Brother, what are you doing? What you are actually saying here is: "Whether you like it or not, you should honor me as a holy person." It would have been preferable if that person recognized your good will and felt ashamed of your humility, asking for your

13. In this case, the word passionate is used by Zosimas to show the intense desire that one is called to direct toward God. However, the term employed here is ὁρμή (*orme* or desire) and not πάθος (*pathos* or passion)

14. *Life of Antony*, ch. 20.

forgiveness. Therefore, as a disciple of the meek and humble one (Matt. 11.29), pay the toll and move on peacefully.'"

b.     On another occasion, when I happened to be in the Holy City [of Jerusalem],[15] a lay Christian approached me and said: "My brother and I have had a slight argument, but he does not wish to be reconciled with me. Please exhort him by speaking to him." I was very glad to accept this request, and called the brother in order to speak to him about the meaning of love and peace. He seemed to be persuaded, but then he told me that he could not be reconciled with his brother because he had sworn by the cross. I smiled and told him: "Your oath is like saying to Christ that, by His precious cross, you will not keep His commandments but instead prefer to perform the will of His enemy, the devil. For, not only are we not obliged to keep to something that was wrongly decided, but also we should rather repent and grieve over our wrong decision, as the God-bearing Basil states.[16] For, indeed, had even Herod repented and not kept his oath, he would not have fallen into that great sin of beheading the Forerunner of Christ." Then, I proceeded to quote for him the passage from Saint Basil, wherein he commented on the Gospel words that the Lord desired to wash the feet of Saint Peter, and the latter objected (cf. John 13.1-11).[17]

## IX. On Spiritual Discipline

a.     The blessed Abba Zosimas also said: "I was once asked how one should control one's anger. And I responded: 'The beginning of controlling one's anger is not speaking when one is troubled. This is why Abba Moses was not troubled, although he was despised by those who told him: "What are you doing among us, you Ethiopian?" He simply said: "Although I was troubled, I did not speak" (Psalm 118.60). The second thing that Abba Moses did was that, not only was he not troubled, but he even rebuked himself saying: "Your skin is as black as ashes. You are not a man, so why should you be allowed to be among other people?" '"[18]

---

15. Moschus, *Spiritual Meadow*, ch. 216 (PG 87: 3108).
16. *Letter 199 to Amphilochius*, ch. 29 (PG 32: 725).
17. *Short Rules* 60 (PG 31: 1122). See also *On the Judgment of God* 7 (PG 32: 672).
18. *Sayings*, Moses 3-4.

b.　　We, however, are very much inferior to Abba Moses, for we cannot even attain to the beginner's stage on account of our great neglect; and so we think that these commandments are immense and impossible. For, to be troubled and not to speak is not for those who are perfect, but for beginners. What is truly great is not to be troubled at all, according to the holy prophet who said: "I was put to shame, but was not troubled" (Psalm 118.60). Yet, we do not seek to make a beginning in this; nor again do we even show any desire toward it, in order to attract God's grace for our assistance. Indeed, even when we think we are showing some desire, it is actually luke-warm and worthless, undeserving to receive anything good from God.

c.　　Everything that we do in the spiritual life is like the seed and the crop. We offer our free will, and we receive from grace. It is like the farmer who sows a little, but with God's pleasure reaps a great deal for his labor. As it is written about Isaac, he sowed in that land and harvested barley one hundredfold during that year (Gen. 26.12). So also, if God blesses our free will, we are able to achieve everything dispassionately, effortlessly and comfortably. For, making an effort to pray and to endure produces pure and comfortable prayer. Moreover, forcing our free will to act brings the action of grace comfortably.

d.　　We can see the same thing happening in every craft. For, when someone approaches a master in order to learn a craft, at the beginning one toils and is clumsy, sometimes even destroying one's work. Nevertheless, one is not discouraged by this, but simply tries again.[19] Even if the work is destroyed a second time, still one does not give in but shows the master one's attempts. In fact, if one is discouraged and gives up, then one learns nothing at all. If one destroys the work many times but does not give up, instead persisting in one's labor and work, then one will learn the technique with God's grace and will start doing everything easily and confidently, to the point where one may even make a living from it.

e.　　The same applies to spiritual work. If one undertakes the task of acquiring virtue, one should not imagine that one might achieve this immediately; for, this is impossible. Rather, one should make an

19. Dorotheus, *Instruction* VIII, 94.

effort, and not give up if it does not work out, simply because one cannot achieve something. Instead, one should try again, just like the one who wants to learn a craft. Moreover, by being very patient and not being discouraged, God will recognize one's labor of desire and grant that one be able to do everything effortlessly. This is what is meant by the words of Abba Moses: "The strength of those who wish to acquire the virtues lies in this: that, should they fall, they do not lose heart, but stand up and try again."[20]

## X. On Avoiding Neglect and on Acquiring Grace

a.    He used to say: "Every virtue requires labor, and time, and our desire, and above all God's cooperation. For, if God does not coop- erate with our free will, then our struggle is in vain. It is like the farmer, who cultivates and sows his land, but God does not rain on his seed.[21] Nevertheless, God's cooperation also requires our prayer and supplication. It is through these that we attract God's assistance for our support. If we neglect prayer, how will God ever recognize our work? Alternatively, how can He do so if we pray in a lukewarm fashion, or in some lazy manner, or if we are quickly discouraged? As I always say: 'Then, we do not deserve to receive anything at all. For, God pays attention to our desire and grants His gifts in accor- dance to this.'"

b.    Was not Abba Moses formerly a chief robber? Did he not do numerous sinful deeds? Did they not even drive him away from his patron because of his bad character? Yet, since he approached his new life courageously, as well as with such fervent desire, we have all seen what spiritual heights he reached, so that he was numbered among the chosen servants of God, according to his biographer.[22]

c.    Yet, in time, through neglect, we lose even the little fervor that we suppose we have in our ascetic renunciation. We become attached to useless, insignificant, and entirely worthless matters, substituting these for the love of God and neighbor, appropriating material things as if they were our own or as if we had not received them from God. "What do you have that you did not receive? And

20. In Abba Isaiah, *Ascetic Discourses* 16.
21. Abba Dorotheus, *Instruction* XII, 135-136.
22. Palladius, *Lausiac History*, ch. 19.

if you received it, then why do you boast as if it were not a gift?" (1 Cor. 4.7).

d.     He also said: "Is our Lord so poor, that He cannot grant us every good, in the same way as He rendered the holy Patriarchs wealthy? If only He truly saw us profiting from whatever He bestowed upon us, then He would do so. However, since He sees that we are harmed by the few and small gifts that He offers us, because of our bad character, He therefore can no longer entrust us with too much, so that we might not be completely destroyed. For, He is loving-kind. Indeed, if He saw that we could profit by the little that we receive from Him, He could easily grant us much more, as I said. In any case, who was it that persuaded those people to throw the money before the feet of the holy Apostles (Acts 4.35; 37)? Yet, it is as I always say: 'Inasmuch as He is good, God has given us to profit from everything. However, we become attached to and misuse God's gifts; and so we turn these very same good gifts to destruction through our evil choice, and are therefore harmed.'"

e.     He frequently used to say: "No one can harm a faithful soul. Rather, everything that such a soul may suffer is considered by it to be profitable. Whereas an unfaithful soul is condemned by its faith-lessness, like a laborer who receives one's reward after toiling. A faithful soul, which remains faithful throughout the labor and expects to be rewarded for its endurance, will receive great comfort. On the other hand, the unfaithful soul, which does not expect to receive the Lord's reward, will find no consolation. So it simply sits and decays in its own thoughts, dwelling on whatever small matter occurs: 'He said this to me.' Or: 'I will say this to him.' That person bears grudges and imagines impossible matters, which he very often cannot bring to fruition. For, people cannot do whatever they imagine, but only what God allows them to do and for the reasons that God alone knows."

f.     Often, one endeavors to do some injustice to another person, but if God does not permit this to happen, the intention is brought to nothing. In that case, people's intentions are merely being tested. How many people tried to hurt the holy Patriarchs, but these latter came to no harm because God did not permit this to happen. For, it is written: "He allowed no one to oppress them; He rebuked kings on their account, saying, 'Do not touch my anointed ones; do my prophets no harm'" (Psalm 104.14-15). Indeed, when He wants to reveal the measure of His power, He is even able to stir to compassion the hearts of the merciless. As it is written in the book of Daniel: "Now the Lord allowed Daniel to receive favor and compassion from the palace master" (Dan. 1.9).

g.     Truly blessed is the soul that, through its thirst for God, is prepared to receive His gifts. For, God will in no way abandon that soul, but will always support it, even in those matters where, out of ignorance, the soul does not approach God. That wise man was right in saying: "God protects a wise person." How many times did Saul attempt to kill the blessed David? What did the former not try? What did he not scheme? Yet, because the Lord protected David, every conspiracy of Saul was brought to nothing. Not only this, but Saul was even delivered into the hands of the holy David, who actually spared him (1 Sam. 24). For David was neither embittered nor provoked by evil.

h.     Someone asked Abba Zosimas: "How can one be despised and abused by other people and yet not become angry?" He replied: "If one considers oneself as being worthless, then one will not be troubled. As Abba Poemen said: 'If you take little account of yourself, then you will have peace.'"[23]

## XI. The Patience of Abba Zosimas

a.     He used to say: "One day, one of the brothers who lived with me and who received the monastic tonsure from me, and for this reason also received careful spiritual formation from me—for he was very sensitive, and I would make concessions for his weakness—told me: : 'My Abba, I love you very much.' And I replied: 'I have yet to find someone who loves me as much as I love that person. Now you are saying that you love me, and I am convinced. However, if something happens, which you do not like, you will not have the same sentiment. Whereas I, no matter what I come to suffer from you, cannot be separated from your love by anything at all.'"

b.     A short time passed, and I cannot remember what actually happened to that brother. However, he began to say many things against me, and I would hear that he even spoke shamelessly about

23. *Sayings*, Poemen 81.

me. Nevertheless, I would say to myself: "This is the brandishing fire of Jesus, and it has been sent to me in order to heal my vainglorious soul. From such things, one may gain much profit, whereas one gains only harm from those who praise us. Truly, such a person is a benefactor." Moreover, I would remember that brother as being my doctor and benefactor. So I would tell my informants: "He only knows my visible wrongdoings, and even those he does not know completely but only partly. As for the invisible wrongs, they are innumerable."

c.      Then, some time afterward, the brother met me in Caesarea. He approached me to greet me and to embrace me in the usual manner. I responded in the same way, as if nothing had occurred.[24] And, although he had said all these things about me, whenever he would encounter me, he would always warmly greet me and I would not give him the slightest indication at all of any remaining sorrow, even though I would continue to hear about what he used to say.

d.      Yet, one day, he fell down before me and held my legs, saying: "Forgive me, my Abba, for the Lord's sake; for, I have said many terrible things against you." I embraced him warmly and told him in a humorous manner: "Does your love remember telling me how much you loved me? Do you remember how I responded, that I had not yet found anyone who could love me as much as I loved that person? Do you recall my words that, if something should happen, which you would not like, you might not have the same sentiment; whereas I, no matter what I would suffer from you, could never be separated from your love by anything at all? You may rest assured in your heart, that nothing of what you have said has escaped me. I have heard everything concerning where and to whom you have spoken. I never once imagined that this was not the case. Nor did anyone persuade me to say anything evil against you. Rather, I would tell them that what my brother says is true, and he is speaking out of love for my sake. In addition, I would never forget you in my prayers. In fact, in order to give you some evidence of my love, once when I hurt my eye badly, I remembered you and made the sign of the cross, saying: 'Lord Jesus Christ, heal me through my brother's

---

24. Pavlos Evergetinos adds: "This happened not simply once or twice, but many times." The Armenian text also reads: "We would exchange friendly conversation for a long time."

prayers.' And I was immediately healed." That is what I told the brother.[25]

e.     Often the blessed Abba Zosimas would say: "We human beings do not know how to be loved or how to be honored. We have lost our sense of balance. For, if someone endures one's brother even a little, when the latter is angry or afflicted, then when that brother comes to his senses and recognizes how the other has endured him, he would give his own life for that person."

## XII. On Meekness and Patience in Affliction

a.     The blessed Abba Zosimas also remembered that someone once told him of a very meek Old Man, saying that because of his great virtue and the wonders that he performed, the entire land regarded him as an angel of God. Therefore, one day, someone was incited by the enemy and came to insult that Old Man in the worst possible manner, in the presence of everyone. The Old Man stood up and simply pointed to that person's mouth, saying: "The grace of God is in your mouth, my brother." The latter was further outraged and said: "Sure, you wicked and hoary old glutton. You are just saying this in order to pretend to others that you are meek." The Old Man responded: "That is true, my brother; what you are saying is the truth." After all this, it is said, someone else asked the Old Man: "Good monk, were you not troubled just now?" He replied: "No. In fact, I felt that my soul was being protected by Christ." And the blessed Abba Zosimas added: "It is true that one ought to give thanks for these things and, if one is indeed filled with passions, to regard such people as doctors who heal the wounds of the soul; and if one is dispassionate, one should regard them as benefactors who procure for us the heavenly kingdom."[26]

b.     That blessed Abba Zosimas again used to say: "When I was still in the monastery in Tyre, before I had left that place, a certain virtuous Old Man came to visit us.[27] We were reading *The Sayings of the Holy Fathers.*" For, the blessed Zosimas always loved to read these *Say-*

---

25. Pavlos Evergetinos adds: "From that time, the brother completely trusted in me and stopped speaking against me, instead esteeming and loving me greatly."

26. Abba Dorotheus, *Letter* IX, 194.

27. John Moschus, *Spiritual Meadow*, ch. 212 (PG 87: 3104-3105).

*ings* all the time; they were almost like the air that he breathed. It is from these *Sayings* that he came to receive the fruit of every virtue. So he said the following: "We came to the passage where the Old Man was robbed by thieves,[28] who said to him: 'We have come to take everything in your cell,' and he replied: 'Children, take whatever you think you should take.' So they took everything and departed, leaving behind a small sack. Then, the Old Man, as it is written, 'took the sack and ran after the thieves, crying out to them: "Children, take also this, which you left behind in my cell." And they were so astonished at the guilelessness of the Old Man, that they returned everything to his cell, repented and said to one another: "Truly, this is a man of God!" '"

c.    Therefore, when we read this passage, the visiting Old Man said to me: "Do you understand this saying, my dear Abba? It has been of great benefit to me." I asked him: "How so?" He replied: "Once, when I was living in the region beside the Jordan, I read this passage and admired the Old Man, saying: 'Lord, make me worthy to follow in the footsteps of this man, since you counted me worthy to wear the same monastic habit.' Thus, while I still had this longing, two days later, behold, thieves broke into my cell. So, as they struck at the door and I understood that they were thieves, I said to myself: 'Thanks be to God! Behold, it is time to prove the fruit of my longing.' I opened the door and received them with gladness; I lit a lamp and began to show them my possessions, telling them: 'Do not worry, I trust in the Lord, and I shall not conceal anything from you.' They asked me: 'Do you have any gold?' I replied: 'Yes, I do, I have three gold coins.' And I opened the box before them, they took the gold and left peacefully." As for me, the blessed Abba said, I asked the Old Man in humor: "Did the thieves return, like they did in the story of the other Old Man?" He replied immediately: "May God never allow this. I would not want this to happen, namely that they might return."

d.    And Abba Zosimas concluded: "Look at the longing and the readiness of that Old Man. Look at what he received as a result. Not only was he not grieved, but in fact he even rejoiced that he was made worthy of such good. Indeed, since I have remembered this

---

28. *Apophthegmata*, Nau no. 337.

story," Zosimas said, "in telling you all that I have said, how by enduring our troubled brother just a little, we can even gain his soul, I would also like to tell you a story that I heard from the blessed Abbot Sergius in Pedias."

## XIII. The Power of Gentleness

a.     He told me the following story: "Once, when we were traveling with a holy Old Man, we lost our way. Not knowing in which direction we were traveling, we found ourselves in a field that was sown, and we trampled on some of the seed. When the farmer became aware of this—for he happened to be working there—he began to insult us greatly, saying angrily: : 'What sort of monks are you? Do you suppose that you are afraid of God? If you held the fear of God before your eyes, you would not have done this.' So the holy man immediately told us that no one should speak at all. Instead, he replied with meekness: 'You are right, my child. If we possessed the fear of God, we would not have done this.' However, that man again insulted us angrily, and the Old Man once more replied: 'What you say is true; had we been monks, we would not have done this. Yet, for the Lord's sake, forgive us; for, indeed, we are at fault.' The farmer was surprised and came and threw himself before the Old Man's feet, saying: 'Forgive me, for the Lord's sake, and take me with you.' The blessed Sergius would conclude: 'That man truly followed us, and even came to wear the monastic habit.'"

b.     The blessed Abba Zosimas added: "Look at what the meekness and good will of the saint were able to achieve, with God's grace, for the salvation of a person created in the image of God, which God desires more so than thousands of worlds and riches."

c.     Once, when I was visiting him, he told me: "Read us a passage from Scripture." Now, as I commenced to read from the book of Proverbs, I came to the passage where it is written: "Where there is an abundance of wood, the fire burns; and where there is no anger, quarreling ceases" (Prov. 26.20).[29] So I asked him: "What does this passage mean, Father?" He replied: "The wood causes the fire to burn. For lack of wood, however, the fire will go out. So it is, also,

29. See Abba Dorotheus, *Instruction* VIII, 91.

with the causes of passions. If one cuts off these causes, then the passions are not active. For example, the causes of fornication are, as Abba Moses said, 'eating and drinking excessively, too much sleep, being idle and jesting and chattering, embellishment of clothes.' And again, the causes of anger are, according to the same person, 'giving and taking, doing one's own will, loving to teach, and considering oneself as being prudent.'[30] Therefore, if one cuts these off, then the passions are weakened. This is what Abba Sisoes meant, when he responded to a brother's question about why the passions do not leave us. He said: 'Their tools, namely their causes, are still inside you. Give them their due pledge, and they will go.'"[31]

d.     A person of dissent, in whom quarrel is not calmed, is a person who is never content with being troubled once, but provokes himself to anger a second time. The opposite kind of person will come to himself when provoked to anger and will blame himself, approaching the brother against whom he was angered in order to repent. Such a person is not a person of dissent. For, quarrel is calmed within this person. Such a person will accuse himself, and be reconciled with his brother, so that there will be no room for quarrel within, as I have already said. On the other hand, someone who is angry but does not blame himself, prefers rather to be provoked to anger and regrets not so much the anger as such, but not having said more against his brother than what was already spoken in turmoil. Such a person is called a dissenter. In such a person, quarrel is never calmed. For, anger is succeeded by grudge, and sorrow, and evil. May the Lord Jesus Christ deliver us of this kind, and make us worthy to be with the meek and humble.

e.     Abba Zosimas often used to say: "We require great vigilance and much prudence in order to face the variety of the devil's evil. For, there are times when the devil will cause someone to be troubled out of nothing; and there are other times when the devil will propose a reasonable excuse, in order that one may suppose that one was justly angered for a good reason. Nevertheless, for someone who truly longs to travel the way of the saints, this is completely foreign, as Saint Macarius says: 'It is not proper for monks to become

---

30. See Abba Isaiah, *Ascetic Discourses* 7
31. *Sayings*, Sisoes 6. See also Abba Dorotheus, *Instruction* XIII, 141.

angry, just as it is inappropriate for monks to grieve their neighbor.'"[32]

f.    He also used to say: "Once, I commissioned certain books to a brilliant calligrapher. When he had completed his work of writing, he sent me a message saying: 'I have finished my work. Whenever you want, send someone to pick them up.' When one of the brothers heard about this, he went to the calligrapher in my name, paid him the money and took the books. Since I was unaware of this, I sent one of our other brothers with a letter and the payment in order for the books to be picked up. Now, when the calligrapher understood that he was deceived by the first brother, who had already picked them up, he was troubled and said: 'Indeed, I am going to be disgusted with that brother in two ways: both because he tricked me, as well as because he took what did not belong to him.' When I heard this, I sent him a message saying: 'My brother, you know that we acquire books in order to learn from them about love, humility and meekness. If the beginning of acquiring books includes quarrel, then I do not want to acquire any books in order to start quarreling. "The Lord's servant must not be quarrelsome" (2 Tim. 2.24).' Thus, by despising the book, I helped the brother not to be troubled at all."

## XIV. On the Subject of Spiritual Gain

a.    The blessed Abba Zosimas used to sit down and talk on the subject of spiritual gain. He would begin by quoting some of the words of the holy Fathers. He came to the saying [in the *Apophthegmata*] by Abba Poemen, namely that one who blames himself finds rest in everything.[33] He also came to the saying [in the *Apophthegmata*] by the Abba of the Nitrian mountain who was asked what more he had found in his particular way of living. He replied that he had learned to accuse and blame himself at all times, to which the person asking the question added: "There is no other way but this."[34] And Abba Zosimas would say: "What power is contained in

32. Saying preserved in the Coptic: Am 171, 16 (*Sentences des Pères*, suppl. Solesmes, 1976), p. 176. See Dorotheus, *Instruction* II, 29 and VIII, 89, where he attributes this saying to Evagrius.

33. *Sayings*, Poemen 95 and 134. See Dorotheus, *Instruction* VII, 81.

34. *Sayings*, Theophilus 1. See Dorotheus, *Instruction* VII, 81.

the words of the saints! Truly, whatever they said, they spoke out of experience and truth, as the sacred Antony also says.[35] Their words were powerful because they spoke of what they practiced; as one of the sages put it: 'May your life confirm your words!'"[36]

b.    Abba Zosimas also used to relate the following story: "During a brief stay at the monastery of Abba Gerasimus, there was a particular brother that I loved. As we were sitting one day and speaking on the subject of spiritual gain, I recalled these words by Abba Poemen and the other elder, and he said to me: 'I am experienced in the truth of these words and in the rest that they refer to. For, once, I had a deacon, who was a truly dear friend in the monastery, and for some reason, which I cannot remember now, he held me in suspicion in regard to some matter that caused him sorrow. Therefore, he began to look sadly toward me. When I noticed him looking gloomy, I asked to find out the reason for this, and he told me: "You did such and such a thing." I was unaware of having done anything like this at all. Nevertheless, I began to offer him assurance in this regard. He said to me: "Forgive me, but I am not convinced." Then I departed for my cell and began to examine my heart as to whether I had done any such thing, but I could not find anything. Afterward, I saw him holding the chalice in his hand, distributing Communion to the brothers; and I swore to him on the chalice that I was not conscious of doing anything of the like. Still, he was not persuaded.

c.    "'Coming once again to myself, I recalled these words of the holy Fathers. Indeed trusting in them, I gradually converted my thought and said to myself: "The deacon loves me genuinely, and it is out of this love that he was moved to confide in me whatever his heart felt in my regard, so that I might be vigilant and more careful from now on. Nevertheless, wretched soul, since you say that you have not done any such thing, you have in any case committed thousands of wrongs, which you have already forgotten. Where are all those things, which you did yesterday or ten days ago? Can you even remember them? Therefore, you must have done this wrong too, just as you did those; and you must have forgotten about this too, just as you forgot about those." In this way, I disposed my heart to

---

35. *Life of Antony,* ch. 39.
36. Moschus, *Spiritual Meadow,* ch. 219 (PG 87: 3109-3112).

say that I truly did do this but had forgotten about it, just as I forgot about my former wrongdoings. Moreover, I began to give thanks to God and to the deacon. For, through him, the Lord made me worthy to recognize my error and to repent of it. Therefore, rising with these thoughts, I came to the deacon in order to repent and in order to thank him. And, as I knocked on his door, he opened and first made a prostration before me, saying: "Forgive me, for I have been deceived by the demons, suspecting that you did that thing. In truth, however, God has assured me that you did nothing of the sort.'" And the brother added: 'He did not even permit me to assure him, but instead said: "It is not necessary."'"

d.      The blessed Abba Zosimas also said: "Such is genuine humility. It disposed the heart of the one who longed for it not only in order not to scandalize the deacon or be grieved toward him, first for suspecting him and second for not being convinced by him when he tried to persuade him. Yet, humility even made the heart ascribe the error to himself. In fact, what is more than this, it made the brother additionally give thanks to the other."

Abba Zosimas added: "Can you see what virtue does? Do you see how many degrees of progress it holds for the one who desires it? For, had he so wanted, he could have had thousands of excuses to act as a demon toward the deacon. Nevertheless, since he was disposed toward virtue, not only did he not grieve over what had happened, but he even thanked the deacon in addition; for, virtue had seized his heart. So it is also with us. If we are in timely fashion and dispose our heart modestly in the seeds of meekness and humility, then the enemy would have no room to sow evil seeds in the heart. However, because the enemy finds our heart deserted of every good thought, and even finds us inciting ourselves toward evil, this is why he seizes these opportunities from us and fulfils his work in order for the opposite to occur from what happens in the case of virtue. For, when virtue sees the soul thirsting for salvation and cultivating good seeds, then it too fulfils its gifts when it sees the willingness of the soul."

## XV. On Perfect Detachment

a.      Once, Abba Zosimas remembered the saying about the Old Man, who was robbed by his neighboring brother. Instead of ever rebuking his brother, that Old Man began to work harder, thinking that the brother had need of these.[37] Abba Zosimas admired the compassion of the saints, and also told the following story.

b.    "Once, when I was at Pedias, an Abbot told me this story:[38] 'There was an Old Man, who lived near our monastery and who had a very good soul. There was another brother, who also lived nearby. When the Old Man was absent one day, that brother was tempted to open the Old Man's cell, enter inside, and take his vessels and books. So when the Old Man returned, he opened the door and, not finding his vessels, he went to announce this to the brother. However, he found his vessels still lying in the middle of the brother's cell; for, the brother had not yet put them away. Not wishing to put the brother to shame or to rebuke him, he pretended that he had a stomachache and went to the toilet for enough time so as to allow the brother to put away the vessels. Then, the Old Man returned and began to speak with the brother on another subject. He did not rebuke the brother at all. After a few days, however, the Old Man's vessels were recognized, and the brother was taken to prison without the Old Man knowing anything about it. When he heard about the brother, namely that he was in prison, he was still unaware of the reason for which the brother was imprisoned. So he came to me,' said the Abbot, 'for he would frequently visit us, and said: "Please, be so kind as to give me some eggs and some church bread." I asked him: "Do you have visitors coming today?" He said: "Yes." However, the Old Man wanted these in order to visit the prison and bring some consolation to the brother. Now, when he entered the prison, the brother fell to his feet and said: "I am here on account of you, Abba. For, I am the one who stole your vessels. Nevertheless, here, take your book; it is here. And take this clothing; it is yours." The Old Man told him: "Child, may your heart be assured, that this is not the reason I came here. I did not know at all that you are here because of me. Nevertheless, on hearing that you are here, I was saddened. Therefore, I have come to bring you some consolation. Look, here are some eggs and some church bread. Now, then, I shall do all that I can in order to have you removed from prison." Indeed, the Old Man went off and begged

37. *Apophthegmata*, Nau no. 339.
38. Moschus, *Spiritual Meadow*, ch. 211 (PG 87: 3101-3104).

certain dignitaries—for, he was well known among them because of his virtue—and they arranged for the brother to come out of prison.'"

c.     "Again, they also used to say the following about the same Old Man. Once he went to the market place in order to purchase some clothing for himself. And he bought it. Having given a piece of gold, he still had to pay some small change. So he took the clothing and placed it beneath him. While he was counting out the coins on the counter, someone came along and wanted to steal the clothing. The Old Man perceived this and understood what was happening. Yet, since he had a merciful and compassionate heart, he lifted himself up gradually, supposedly pretending to reach out over the counter in order to pay the coins. In this way, the other person was able to steal the clothing, and departed. The Old Man, however, did not rebuke him."

d.     And the blessed Abba Zosimas would conclude: "How expensive were the clothing and the vessels, which the Old Man had lost? Yet, his great will power revealed that he possessed these material things without any attachment to them. He neglected the fact that they had been stolen, and simply remained the same person; he was neither saddened nor troubled. For, as I always like to say: 'It is not possessing something that is harmful, but being attached to it.' Even if this Old Man possessed the whole world, he would have done so without being attached to it. From his actions, he proved that he was free from everything."

\*

\*   \*

Therefore, brothers, let us, too, struggle to imitate with eagerness the words of the holy Fathers in order that we may bear fruit and inherit the eternal goods. In Christ Jesus our Lord, to whom be the glory and the power, together with the Father and the Holy Spirit, now and always, and to the ages of ages. Amen.[39]

\*

\*   \*

39. From the conclusion to the text (PG 78: 1701).

# From the Teachings of Abba Dorotheus
## on Abba Zosimas

Once, Abba Zosimas was speaking about humility.[40] A sophist happened to be there, listening to what Zosimas was saying, and he wanted to find out the exact meaning of his words. So he asked him: "Tell me. How is it that you regard yourself as being a sinner? Do you not know that you are a saint? Do you not know that you have many virtues? Surely, you can see how you practice the commandments! How can you do these things, and yet regard yourself as being a sinner?" The Old Man could not find the proper way of wording his response. Nevertheless, he said: "I do not know what to say to you in response. However, that is how I regard myself." Therefore, the sophist argued with him, wanting to learn how this could be so. Yet, the Old Man still could not find a way of explaining this to him, and began to respond with his holy simplicity: "Do not torment me; I just know that this is the case."

When I noticed that the Old Man was unsure as to how to reply, I told him: "Is it not the same, I wonder, in sophistry and medicine? When someone learns this art well and practices it, gradually, by exercising it, it becomes like a second nature to the doctor or the sophist. Then, such people cannot explain or express how this habit occurred gradually, as I said, and how imperceptibly it has seized their soul, simply by practicing the art. The same also happens in the case of humility. For, from the keeping of the commandments, a certain habitual humility occurs, which cannot be explained in words."

When Abba Zosimas heard this, he was pleased and immediately embraced me, saying: "You are right. That is exactly how it is. It is just as you have said it." The sophist too was satisfied with the response and admitted that this was the reason.

Abba Zosimas said:[41] "Even if the devil, working together with all of his demons, places in action all the machinations of his evil, all these strategies are in vain and are brought to nothing, according to the command of Christ, by humility."

---

40. In Abba Dorotheus, *Instruction* II, 36.
41. Saying of Abba Zosimas, cited by Dorotheus, *Instruction* VIII, 94.

# Appendix

## Give me a Word, Abba

The brief sayings that follow, from the *Alphabetical Collection*, not otherwise used throughout the book, are selected here and presented, in a fresh translation, intended for general reading and personal meditation.

### Abba Antony

7. Abba Antony said: "I saw all the snares of the enemy spread out over the world and I sighed wondering who could ever escape such snares. Then I heard a voice, saying to me: 'Humility.'"

17. One day, some of the old men came to visit Abba Antony. Among them was Abba Joseph. Wanting to test them, the old man proposed a text from Scripture and asked them, beginning with the youngest, to explain it. Each one offered his opinion to the degree that he could. But to each of them, the old man said: "You did not understand it." Lastly, he turned to Abba Joseph, saying: "How would you explain this saying?" Abba Joseph replied: "I do not know." Then Abba Antony said: "Truly, Abba Joseph has found the way; for, he said: 'I do not know.'"

### Abba Arsenius

5. Someone once asked the blessed Arsenius: "Abba, how is it that, with all our education and breadth of knowledge, we get nowhere, whereas these Egyptian peasants acquire so many virtues?" Abba Arsenius replied: "We indeed gain nothing from our secular learning, but these Egyptian peasants acquire virtues through hard work."

10. He also said: "If we seek God, he will reveal Himself to us; and if we keep Him, He will stay close to us."

*Abba Agathon*

4. The old man said: "I have never gone to sleep with a grievance against anyone; and, as far as I was able, I have never let anyone else go to sleep with a grievance against me."

11. The same Abba Agathon was walking with his disciples. One of them found a small pea on the road and asked the old man: "Father, may I take it?" The old man looked at him with astonishment and replied: "Was it you that put it there?" The brother said: "No." The old man continued: "How then can you pick up something that you did not lay down?"

26. Abba Agathon said: "If I could meet a leper, give him my body and take his, I would be very happy. For, this is indeed perfect love."

27. It was said of him that, upon coming into town one day to sell his manual work, he encountered an ill traveler lying in the public square without anyone to care for him. The old man rented a room and lived there with him, working with his hands in order to pay the rent and spending all of his money on the needs of the sick man. He stayed there for four months until the sick man became healthy. The he returned in peace to his own cell.

*Abba Alonius*

3. The old man said: "If only a person desired it for a single day—from morning to night—that person would be able to reach the measure of God."

*Abba Bessarion*

7. A brother who had sinned was dismissed from the community by the priest. Abba Bessarion stood up and walked out with him, saying: "I, too, am a sinner."

11. At the point of his death, Abba Bessarion said: "A monk ought to be like the Cherubim and the Seraphim: all eye!"

*Abba Epiphanius*

6. The old man said: "The Canaanite woman cries out, and she is heard (Matt. 15); the woman with the issue of blood is silent, and she is called blessed (Luke 8); the Pharisee speaks, and he is condemned (Matt. 9); while the publican does not open his mouth, and he too is heard (Luke 18)."

*Abba Euprepios*

2. The old man helped some thieves when they came to steal from him. When they had taken everything from inside his cell, Abba Euprepios noticed that they had left behind his stick, and he felt sorry. He took the stick and ran after them in order to hand it to them. But the thieves did not wish to take it, fearing that something might happen to them as a result. So the old man asked someone else, whom he met and who was heading in the same direction, to take it to them.

*Abba Isaiah*

8. The old man said: "If someone seeks to render evil for evil, then he can injure his brother's soul even with a single nod of the head."

*Abba Theophilus*

2. Abba Theophilus, the archbishop, came to Scetis one day. The assembled brothers said to Abba Pambo: "Say something to the archbishop so that he may be edified." The old man told them: "If he is not edified by my silence, then he will not be edified by my speech either."

*Amma Theodora*

5. Amma Theodora said that a teacher should be a stranger to the desire for domination, vainglory and pride; one should not be able

to deceive him by flattery or blind him with gifts; one should not easily conquer him by means of food or control him by means of anger. Instead, he should be patient, gentle and humble as far as this is possible; he must also be tested and without partisanship, full of compassion and a lover of souls.

6. She also said that neither asceticism nor vigils nor suffering of any kind can save a person, but only true humility. There was once a hermit, who was able to banish demons. And he asked the demons: "What makes you disappear? Is it fasting?" They replied: "We neither eat nor drink." He asked again: "Is it vigils?" They said: "We do not sleep either." He then asked: "Is it separation from the world?" They responded: "We inhabit the deserts." Finally, he asked: "Then what power makes you disappear?" They said: "Nothing can overcome us except the power of humility." This is why humility alone is victorious over demons.

*Abba John the Dwarf*

39. Abba John the Dwarf said: "A house is not built by starting at the top and working downward. One must begin from the foundations in order to reach the top." They told him: "What do you mean by this saying?" He replied: "The foundation is our neighbor, whom we must win; that is the place to begin. For, all of the commandments of God depend on this one."

*Abba Isidore (of Pelusia)*

4. Abba Isidore said: "Sin alienates us from God and separates us from other people. So we must immediately turn away from sin and pursue virtue, which leads us to God and unites us with each other. Now the definition of virtue and philosophy is: simplicity with prudence."

6. He also said: "The desire for possessions is dangerous and terrible; it knows no end and drives the soul that it controls to the limits of evil. Therefore, let us drive it away forcefully from the outset. For, once it has mastered us, it cannot be overcome."

*Abba Hierax*

1. A brother questioned Abba Hierax, saying: "Give me a word. How can I be saved?" The old man replied: "Sit in your cell. And if you are hungry, eat; if you are thirsty, drink; only do not speak evil of anyone, and you will be saved."

*Abba Macarius (the Great)*

19. They asked Abba Macarius: "How should one pray?" The old man replied: "There is no need to make long discourses; it is enough simply to stretch out one's hands and say: 'Lord, as you will, and as you know, have mercy.' And if the conflict grows fiercer, say: 'Lord, help!' He knows very well what we need and shows us His mercy."

23. A brother came to visit Abba Macarius the Egyptian and said to him: "Abba, give me a word, that I may be saved." So the old man said: "Go to the cemetery and abuse the dead." The brother went there and abused them, throwing stones at them. He returned and told the old man about it. The elder said: "Did they not speak to you?" He replied: "No." The old man then said: "Go back tomorrow and praise them." So the brother went there and praised them, calling them apostles, saints and righteous. He returned to the old man and said: "I went and praised them." The old man replied: "Did they not respond?" The brother said: "No." The old man finally said: "See how you insulted them and they did not reply; and how you praised them and still they did not speak. If you wish to be saved, you must do the same and become like a dead person. Like them, take no account of either scorn or praise, and you will be saved."

36. Abba Macarius said: "If we keep remembering the wrongs done to us by others, then we destroy the power of the remembrance of God. But if we remind ourselves of the evil deeds of demons, then we shall be invulnerable."

*Abba Mios*

3. A soldier asked Abba Mios whether God accepted our repen-

tance. After the old man had taught him various things, he said: "Tell me, my child, if your cloak is torn, do you throw it away?" He replied: "No, I mend it and use it again." The old man told him: "If you are so careful about your cloak, will not God be equally careful about his creature?"

*Abba Nilus*

1. Abba Nilus said: "Everything that you do in revenge against your brother, who has harmed you, will come back to haunt you at the time of prayer."

2. He also said: "Prayer is the seed of gentleness and the absence of anger."

3. He also added: "Prayer is the antidote for grief and depression."

4. He also said: "Do not always want everything to turn out as you think it should, but rather as God pleases; then you will be undisturbed and grateful in your prayer."

*Abba Xanthias*

1. Abba Xanthias said: "The thief was on the cross and was justified by a single word. And Judas was counted among the apostles but lost all his labor in a single night, descending from heaven to hell. Therefore, let no one boast of good works; for, all those who trust in themselves fall."

*Abba Poemen*

12. A brother asked Abba Poemen: "I have committed a grave sin and I want to do penance for three years." The old man said: "That is too much." The brother said: "One year?" The old man again said: "That is too much." Those present asked: "Forty days?" Again he said: "That is too much." Then he added: "I believe that if someone repents with his whole heart and does not intend to commit the sin any longer, God will accept his repentance after only three days."

29. Abba Poemen said: "If three men meet, the first of whom maintains inner peace, the second gives thanks to God in illness, and the third serves other people with a pure heart, then these three are doing the same thing."

63. Abba Poemen said: "Teach your mouth to say what lies in your heart."[1]

85. Abba Poemen said about Abba Pior that each day he made a new beginning.

121. He also said: "The wickedness of people is concealed behind their backs."

143. A brother visited Abba Poemen and asked: "What should I do?" The old man replied: "Go and find someone who asks: 'What do I want?' and you will find peace."

157. Abba Poemen said: "Instructing your neighbor is the same thing as reproving him."

192. He also said: "There is a voice that cries out to each person until his last breath: 'Be converted today!'"

200. He also said: "Not understanding what happened prevents us from making progress."

*Abba Pambo*

10. Abba Pambo said: "If you have a heart, you can be saved."

*Abba Silvanus*

11. Abba Moses asked Abba Silvanus: "Can a person lay a new foundation every day?" The old man replied: "If one works hard, one

---

1. Also *Saying* 164. *Saying* 188: "Teach your heart to guard that which your tongue teaches."

can lay a new foundation at every moment."

*Abba Sarmatas*

1. Abba Sarmatas said: "I prefer a sinful man, who knows that he has sinned and repents, to a man who has not sinned and considers himself righteous."

*Abba Serapion*

2. A brother said to Abba Serapion: "Give me a word." The old man replied: "What can I tell you? You have taken the living of the widows and orphans, and put it on your shelves." For, he saw that they had many books.

*Abba Hyperechios*

4. Abba Hyperechios said: "It is better to eat meat and drink wine than to eat the flesh of one's neighbor through slander."

# Chronological Table

| | |
|---|---|
| Agathon | d. 370 |
| Ammoun | d. 350 |
| Antony | 251-356 |
| Arsenius | c.354-c.449 |
| Athanasius of Alexandria | c.296-373 |
| Augustine of Hippo | 354-430 |
| Barsanuphius | d.c.543 |
| Basil of Caesarea | 330-379 |
| Cyril of Scythopolis | fl.c. 524-558 |
| Dorotheus of Gaza | c.506-c.570 |
| Ephrain the Syrian | d. 373 |
| Euthymius | 376-473 |
| Evagrius | c.345-399 |
| Hilarion | c.291-c.371 |
| Isaiah of Scetis | d.c.489 |
| Jerome | c.341-420 |
| John Cassian | 360-435 |
| John Chrysostom | 347-407 |
| John the Dwarf | c.339-c.407 |
| John of Lycopolis | d.395 |
| John Moschos | 7th century |
| John the "Other Old Man" | d.c.543 |
| Macarius of Alexandria | 293-393 |
| Macarius of Egypt | c.300-c.390 |
| Mark the Monk | 5th century |
| Melanie the Elder | 342-411 |
| Melanie the Younger | 380-c.439 |
| Moses the Ethiopian | d.c.375 |
| Nilus of Ancyra | 5th century |
| Origen of Alexandria | 185-c.254 |
| Pachomius | 292-346 |
| Palladius of Helenopolis | 5th century |
| Pambo | 304-373 |

| | |
|---|---|
| Paul of Thebes | c.235-c.341 |
| Paula the Elder | 347-404 |
| Paula the Younger | b.c.397 |
| Peter the Iberian | d.c.490 |
| Poemen | d.c.449 |
| Porphyry of Gaza | d. 420 |
| Sabas | 439-532 |
| Sarapion of Thmuis | d.c.370 |
| Seridos | d.c.543 |
| Silvanus | d.c.412 |
| Sisoes | d. 429 |
| Symeon the Stylite | d. 459 |
| Syncletica | 380-c.460 |
| Theodore the Studite | 759-826 |
| Zeno, of Silvanus | d. 451 |
| Zosimas (of the *Reflections*) | fl. 475-525 |

# The Desert of Egypt, Palestine and Sinai

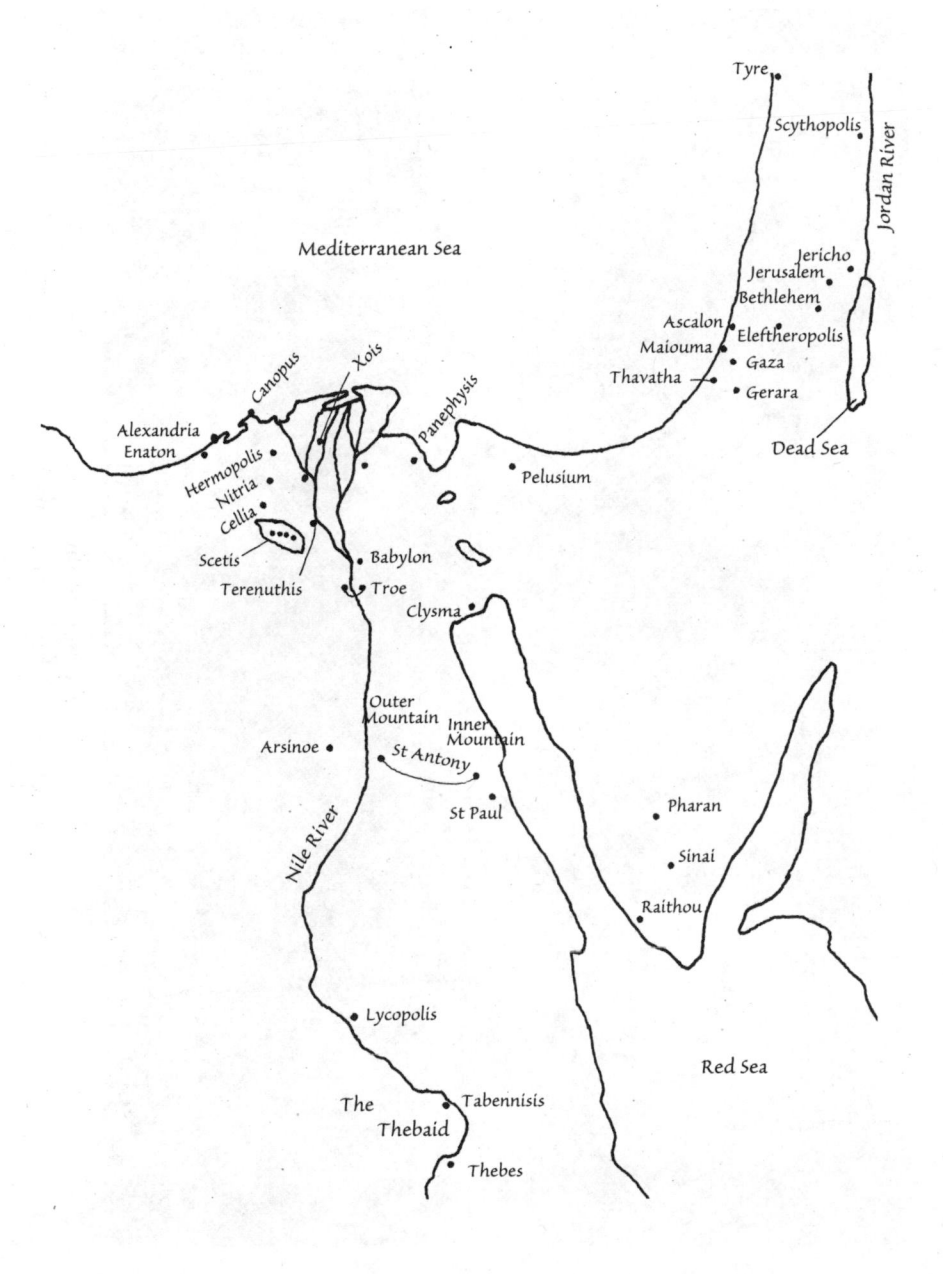

Mediterranean Sea

Tyre
Scythopolis
Jordan River
Jericho
Jerusalem
Bethlehem
Ascalon
Maiouma Eleftheropolis
Thavatha Gaza
Gerara
Dead Sea

Canopus Xois
Panephysis
Alexandria
Enaton
Hermopolis Pelusium
Nitria
Cellia
Scetis Babylon
Terenuthis Troe
Clysma

Outer
Mountain Inner
Mountain
Arsinoe St Antony
St Paul Pharan

Sinai

Raithou

Nile River

Red Sea

Lycopolis

The Tabennisis
Thebaid
Thebes

"The desert is alive"
Oasis in Faran, Mount Sinai

# Bibliography

The following bibliography is divided into original sources and contemporary material. Its primary purpose is to encourage readers to return to the early texts themselves; it also provides further reading on particular subjects raised throughout this book.

## Sources

*Apophthegmata Patrum*. PG 65: 76-440.

——*Vitae Patrum*. PL: 73-74.

——*Revue de l'orient chrétien*.Vols. 10, 12-14, 17-18. The anonymous supplement to the alphabetical collection. Edited by F. Nau. 1905, 1907-09, 1912-13.

——*Patrologia Orientalis*. Vol.VIII, 164-83. Paris, 1912.

——*The Sayings of the Desert Fathers: The Alphabetical Collection*. Translated by B. Ward. Kalamazoo MI: Cistercian Publications, 1975.

——*The Wisdom of the Desert Fathers: Apophthegmata Patrum, The Anonymous Series*. Vol. 48. Translated by B. Ward. Fairacres: Oxford, 1986.

——*The Desert Fathers: Sayings of the Early Christian Monks*. Translated by B. Ward from the Latin collection. Harmondsworth: Penguin, 2003.

——N. Russell. *Lives of the Desert Fathers: the Historia Monachorum in Aegypto*. Kalamazoo: Cistercian Publications, 1981.

Athanasius. *Vita Antonii (The Life of Antony)*. PG 26: 837-976. Translated by R. Gregg. New York: Paulist Press, 1980.

Barsanuphius and John. *Barsanuphius and John: Questions and Answers*. Partial Translation by D.J.Chitty. In *Patrologia Orietalis* XXXI, 3 (1966): 445-616. English translation of the letters of

Barsanuphius and John [forthcoming: Cistercian Publications] by J. Chryssavgis.

Basil the Great. *De judicio Dei.* PG 31: 653-76.

——*Regulae fusius tractatae (Long Rules).* PG 31:889-1052.

——*Regulae brevius tractatae (Short Rules).* PG 31: 1080-1305. See English edition in M. Monica Wagner. *St. Basil: Ascetical Works.* Washington: Catholic University of America Press, 1962.

Cyril of Scythopolis. *Works.* In *Cistercian Studies.* Vol. 114. Translated by R. Price. Kalamazoo MI: Cistercian Publications, 1990.

Dorotheus of Gaza. *Works.* PG 88: 1613-1841. In *Cistercian Studies.* Vol. 33. Translated by E. Wheeler. Kalamazoo MI: Cistercian Publications, 1977.

Evagrius. *Praktikos.* PG 40: 1220-52. In *Cistercian Studies.* Vol. 4. Translated by J.E. Bamburger. Kalamazoo MI: Cistercian Publications, 1970.

——*De octo spiritibus malitiae.* PG 79: 1145-64.

——*De oratione (On Prayer).* PG 79: 1165-2000.

——*De diversis malignis cogitationibus.* PG 79: 1200-33.

——*Centuries.* In *Patrologia Orientalis.* Vol. XXVIII, No. 1. Edited by A. Guillaumont. Paris, 1958.

——*Antirrheticus, Gnosticus, Protrepticus, Paraeneticus,* and *Letters.* In *Evagrius Ponticus.* Edited by W. Frankenberg. Berlin, 1912.

Evergetinos, Paulos. *Synagoge.* Athens, 1957.

*Historia Monachorum In Aegypto.* In N. Russell. *The Lives of the Desert Fathers.* Oxford, 1981.

Ignatius of Antioch. *Letters.* In *The Apostolic Fathers.* Edited by J. Lightfoot. Grand Rapids MI:Baker Book House, 1981.

Isaac the Syrian. *Mystic Treatises by Isaac of Nineveh.* Translated from Bedjan's Syriac text by A. J. Wensinck. Amsterdam, 1923.

Isaiah of Scetis. *Ascetic Discouses.* In *Cistercian Studies.* Vol. 150. Translated by J. Chryssavgis and P.R. Penkett. Kalamazoo MI: Cistercian Publications, 2002.

John Cassian. *Conferences.* Translated by B. Ramsey. New York: Newman Press, 2000.

*Institutions.* Translated by B. Ramsey. New York: Paulist Press, 1997.

——*De octo vitiosis cogitationibus.* PG 79: 1436-72.

John Moschus. *Pratum Spirituale (The Spiritual Meadow).* PG 87, 3:2852-3112. In *Cistercian Studies.* Vol. 139. Translated by J. Wortley. Kalamazoo MI: Cistercian Publications, 1992.

Nilus of Ancyra. *Epistolae.* PG 79: 81-581.

——*Liber de monastica exercitatione.* PG 79: 720-809.

——*De voluntaria paupertate.* PG 79: 968-1060.

——*De monachorum praestantia.* PG 79: 1061-93.

Pachomius. *Pachomian Koinonia.* In *Cistercian Studies.* Vol. 45-46. Translated by A. Veilleux. Kalamazoo, MI: Cistercian Publications, 1980-1.

Palladius. *Lausiac History.* In *Texts and Studies* VI. 2 volumes. Edited by C. Butler. Cambridge, 1898-1904; see also R.T. Meyer. *Ancient Christian Writers.* Vol. 34. Washington DC, 1965.

Theodoret of Cyrrhus. *Philotheos Historia.* In *Sources chrétiennes.* No's. 234 and 257. Edited by P. Canivet and A. Leroy-Molinghen. Paris, 1977-1979.

Zosimas. *Reflections.* In L. Regnault. *Enseignements des Pères du Désert.* Bégrolles-en-Mauges: Abbaye de Bellefontaine, 1991.

## General Bibliography

Aries, P., and A. Bejin, eds. *Western Sexuality. Practice and Precept in Past and Present Times.* Oxford, 1985.

Baynes, N.H. "St. Antony and the Demons." *Journal of Egyptian Archaeology* 40 (1954): 7-10.

Beasley-Topliffe, K., ed. *Seeking a Purer Christian Life: Sayings and Stories of the Desert Fathers and Mothers.* Nashville: Upper Room Books, 2000.

Binns, J. *Ascetics and Ambassadors of Christ: The Monasteries of Palestine 314-631.* Oxford: Clarendon Press, 1994.

Bondi, R. *To Pray and to Love: Conversations on Prayer with the Early Church.* Minneapolis: Fortress Press, 1991.

Bousset, W. *Apophthegmata. Studien zur Geschichte des ältesten Mönchtums.* Tübingen, 1923.

Bouyer, L. *La vie de S.Antoine. Essai sur la spiritualité du monachisme primitif.* S. Wandrille, 1950.

Brock, S., and S. Harvey, eds. *Holy Women of the Syriac Orient.* Berkeley: University of California Press, 1988.

Brown, P. *The Body and Society: Men, Women and Sexual Renunciation in Early Christianity.* Columbia: Columbia University Press, 1990.

Burton-Christie, D. *The Word in the Desert: Scripture and the Quest for Holiness in Early Christian Monasticism.* Oxford: Oxford University Press, 1993.

Bynum, C. W. *Holy Feast and Holy Fast: The Religious Significance of Food to Medieval Women.* Berkeley: University of California Press, 1987.

Chitty, D. *The Desert a City: An Introduction to the Study of Egyptian and Palestinian Monasticism under the Christian Empire.* London: Mowbrays, 1966.

——*The Letters of St. Antony the Great.* Oxford: Fairacres, 1975.

Chrysostomos (Archimandrite). *The Ancient Fathers of the Desert: Translated Narratives from the Evergetinos on Passions and Perfection in Christ.* Brookline MA: Hellenic College Press, 1980.

Chryssavgis, J. *Soul Mending: The Art of Spiritual Direction.* Brookline: Holy Cross Press, 2000.

Clarke, E. A. *Ascetic Piety and Women's Faith. Essays on Late Ancient Christianity.* Lewiston: Edwin Mellen Press, 1986.

Coakley, S. *Religion and the Body.* Cambridge: Cambridge University Press, 1997.

Colliander, T. *The Way of the Ascetics.* New York: St. Vladimir's Seminary Press, 1985.

Elm, S. *"Virgins of God": The Making of Asceticism in Late Antiquity.* Oxford: Clarendon Press, 1994.

Evdokimov, P. *Ages of the Spiritual Life.* New York: St. Vladimir's Seminary Press, 1998.

Festugière, A.J. *Contemplation et vie contemplative selon Platon.* Paris, 1967.

Foucault, M. *The Use of Pleasure. The History of Sexuality,* 3 volumes. New York: Pantheon Books, 1985.

Gannon, T.M. and G. W. Traub. *The Desert and the City: An Interpretation of the History of Christian Spirituality.* Chicago: Loyola University Press, 1984.

Gillet, L. "The Gift of Tears." *Sobornost* 12 (1937): 5-10.

Goehring, G.E. "The Origins of Monasticism." In *Eusebius, Christianity and Judaism,* edited by H.W. Attridge and G. Hata, 135-155. Leiden, 1992.

——"Through a Glass Darkly: Diverse Images of the *Apotaktikoi(ai)* of Early Egyptian Monasticism." *Semeia* 58 (1992): 25-45.

——*Ascetics, Society and the Desert: Studies in Egyptian Monasticism.* Harrisburg PA: Trinity Press International, 1999.

Gould, G. *The Desert Fathers on Monastic Community.* Oxford: Clarendon Press, 1993.

Gruen, A. *Heaven Begins Within You: Wisdom from the Desert Fathers.* New York: Crossroad Publications, 1999.

Guillaumont, A. *Aux origines du monachisme chrétien.* Bellefontaine: *Spiritualité Orientale* 30, 1979.

Hausherr, I. *La méthode d'oraison hésychaste. Orientalia Christiana Analecta* 9, 2. Rome, 1927.

——"Le traité de l'oraison d'Évagre le Pontique." *R.A.M.* 15 1934): 34-93; 113-70. Revised edition in *Les leçons d'un contemplatif. Le traité de l'oraison d'Évagre le Pontique.* Paris, 1960.

——*Spiritual Direction in the Early Christian East. Cistercian Studies.* Vol. 116. Kalamazoo MI: Cistercian Publications, 1990.

Iredale, S. *The Interior Mountain: Encountering God with the Desert Saints.* Nashville: Abingdon Press, 2000.

Jones, A. *Soul Making: The Desert Way of Spirituality.* San Francisco: Harper and Row, 1985.

Lacarrière, J. *The God-Possessed.* London, 1963.

Lane, B. *The Solace of Fierce Landscapes: Exploring Mountain and Desert Spirituality.* Oxford: Oxford University Press, 1998.

Larchet, J. *Thérapeutique des maladies spirituelles. Une introduction à la tradition ascétique de l'Eglise Orthodoxe.* 3rd ed. Paris: Cerf, 1997.

Lienhard, J.T. "'Discernment of Spirits in the Early Church.'" *Studia Patristica* 17 (1982): 519-22.

Losky, V. *The Mystical Theology of the Eastern Church.* London, 1957.

McGinn, B., J. Meyendorff, and J. Leclerq, eds. *Christian Spirituality: Origins to the Twelfth Century.* New York: Crossroads, 1985.

Mauser, U.W. *Christ in the Wilderness.* London, 1963.

Meredith, A. "Asceticism—Christian and Greek." *Journal of Theological Studies* 27 (1976): 313-332.

Merton, T. *The Wisdom of the Desert: Sayings from the Desert Fathers of the Fourth century.* New York: New Directions, 1973.

Meyendorff, J. *A Study of Gregory Palamas.* London, 1964.

Neame, A. *The Hermitage Within: Spirituality of the Heart.* Kalamazoo MI: Cistercian Publications, 1999.

Nellas, P. *Deification in Christ.* Crestwood NY: St. Vladimir's Press, 1987.

Nomura, Y. *Desert Wisdom: Sayings from the Desert Fathers.* Maryknoll NY: Orbis Books, 2001.

Nouwen, H. *The Way of the Heart: Desert Spirituality and Contemporary Ministry.* New York: Seabury Press, 1981.

Ramfos, S. *Like a Pelican in the Wilderness: Reflections on the Sayings of the Desert Fathers.* Brookline: Holy Cross Press, 2000.

Rapp, C. "Storytelling as Spiritual Communication in Early Greek Hagiography: The Use of *Diegesis.*" *Journal of Early Christian Studies* 6,3 (1988): 431-448.

Rousseau, P. *Ascetics, Authority and the Church in the Age of Jerome and Cassian.* Oxford: Oxford University Press, 1978.

——*Pachomius: The Making of a Community in Fourth Century Egypt.* Berkeley: University of California Press, 1985.

Ruffner, H. *The Fathers of the Desert.* New York: Baker and Scribner, 1850.

Sheils, W. J., ed. *Monks, Hermits, and the Ascetic Tradition.* Padstow: T. J. Press, 1985.

Spidlík, T. *La spiritualité de l'orient chrétien.* Rome, 1978.

Stewart, C. *Cassian the Monk.* Oxford: Oxford University Press, 1998.

——*The World of the Desert Fathers: Stories and Sayings from the Anonymous Series of the Apophthegmata Patrum.* Oxford: Fairacres, 1986.

Swan, L. *Forgotten Desert Mothers: Sayings, Lives and Stories of Early Christian Women.* New York: Paulist Press, 2001.

Veyne, P., ed. *A History of Private Life: From Pagan Rome to Byzantium.* Cambridge, MA: Harvard University Press, 1987.

Vivian, T. *Journeying into God: Seven Early Monastic Lives.* Minneapolis: Fortress Press, 1996.

Waddell, H. *The Desert Fathers.* New York: H. Holt, 1936.

Wallace-Hadrill, D.S. *The Greek Patristic View of Nature.* Manchester, 1968.

Walters, K. *Soul Wilderness: A Desert Spirituality.* New York: Paulist Press, 2001.

Ward, B., ed. *Harlots of the Desert: A Study of Repentance in Early Monastic Studies.* London: Mowbray, 1987.

Ware, K.T. *The Inner Kingdom: Collected Works.* Vol. 1. New York: St. Vladimir's Seminary Press, 2000.

——"The Transfiguration of the Body." In *Sacrament and Image,* edited by A.M. Allchin, 17-32. London: The Fellowship of St. Alban and St. Sergius, 1967.

——"Tradition and Personal Experience in Later Byzantine Theology." *Eastern Churches Review* 3 (1970): 131-41.

——*The Power of the Name. The Jesus Prayer in Orthodox Spirituality.* Oxford, 1974.

——"The Spiritual Father in Orthodox Christianity." *Cross Currents* 24 (1974): 296-313 (-20).

——"Silence in Prayer: the Meaning of Hesychia." In *One Yet Two: Cistercian Studies* 29, edited by B. Pennington, 22-47. Kalamazoo MI: Cistercian Publications, 1976.

Williams, G. *Wilderness and Paradise in Christian Thought.* New York: Harper and Row, 1962.

Wimbush, V. L., ed. *Ascetic Behavior in Greco-Roman Antiquity: A Sourcebook.* Minneapolis: Fortress Press, 1990.

Wimbush, V.L., and R. Valantasis, eds. *Asceticism.* Oxford: Oxford University Press, 1995.

"The desert was a calling"
Monastery of Paul of Thebes, Egypt

# Biographical Notes

**Rev. Dr. John Chryssavgis** was born in Australia (1958), where he matriculated from the Scots College (1975). He received his degree in Theology from the University of Athens (1980), a diploma in Byzantine Music from the Greek Conservatory of Music (1979), and was awarded a research scholarship to St. Vladimir's Theological Seminary (1982). He completed his doctoral studies in Patristics at the University of Oxford (1983).

After several months in silent retreat on Mt Athos, he served as Personal Assistant to the Greek Orthodox Primate in Australia (1984-94) and was co-founder of St. Andrew's Theological College in Sydney (1985), where he was Sub-Dean and taught Patristics and Church History (1986-95). He was also Lecturer in the Divinity School (1986-90) and the School of Studies in Religion (1990-95) at the University of Sydney. In 1995, he moved to Boston, where he was appointed Professor of Theology at Holy Cross School of Theology and directed the Religious Studies Program at Hellenic College until 2002. He established the Environment Office at the same School in 2001. He has also taught as professor of Patristics at Balamand University in Lebanon. Currently, he serves as theological advisor to the Ecumenical Patriarch on environmental issues.

The author of several books and numerous articles in several languages on the Church Fathers and Orthodox Spirituality, Fr. John's most recent publications include *Soul Mending: The Art of Spiritual Direction* (Holy Cross Press, 2000), *In the Footsteps of Christ: Abba Isaiah of Scetis* (SLG Press Oxford, 2001), *The Body of Christ: A Place of Welcome for People with Disabilities* (Light and Life, 2002), *Letters from the Desert: A Selection from Barsanuphius and John* (St. Vladimir's Press, 2003), *Cosmic Grace, Humble Prayer: The Ecological Vision of The Green Patriarch* (Eerdmans, 2003), *Light Through Dark-*

*ness: The Orthodox Tradition* (Orbis Books, 2004), *John Climacus: From the Egyptian Desert to the Sinaite Mountain* (Ashgate, 2004), *The Ecumenical Patriarchate: A Brief Guide* (Ecumenical Patriarchate, 2005), *The Reflections of Abba Zosimas* (SLG Press Oxford, 2006), and *Beyond the Shattered Image: Insights into an Orthodox Christian Ecological Worldview* (Light and Life, 2nd ed. 2007). Two volumes with the full correspondence of Barsanuphius and John appeared in 2006-2007 in the Fathers of the Church series of Catholic University Press.

He lives with his family in Bath, Maine.


**Benedicta Ward** is a member of the Community of the Sisters of the Love of God, an Anglican community whose mother house is in Oxford. She is a teaching member of the theology faculty and Reader in the History of Christian Spirituality at the University of Oxford. Sr. Benedicta is the author of many books on medieval topics and has also translated, among other early monastic texts, *The Sayings of the Desert Fathers* (Mowbrays-Cistercian Publications, 1975) and *The Wisdom of the Desert Fathers* (SLG Press, 1975). Her newest book, *The Desert Fathers: Sayings of the Early Christian Monks* was published by Penguin in 2003.


**The Most Reverend Metropolitan Kallistos (Ware) of Diokleia** is an auxiliary bishop of the Ecumenical Patriarchate in Great Britain. Born in Bath, Somerset, England in 1934, throughout his life he has been a leading author and translator of Orthodox texts. He studied Classics and Theology at Magdalene University, Oxford and after traveling through Greece and other Orthodox centers he was ordained to the priesthood in 1966. He held a lecturer position at Oxford in Eastern Orthodox Studies for 35 years until his retirement in 2001. Since his retirement, Metropolitan Kallistos has served as the chairman of the board of directors of the Institute for Orthodox Christian Studies in Cambridge and is currently the chairman of Friends of Orthodoxy in Iona. His best known works include *The Orthodox Church* and *The Orthodox Way,* and his translation of the *Philokalia* with G. E. Palmer and Philip Sherrard.

# Index

Pages 111-150 refer to an included translated text, the *Reflections*, by Abba Zosimas. Pages 151-158 refer to *Appendix: Give me a Word, Abba.*

For a glossary of all key foreign words used in books published by World Wisdom, including metaphysical terms in English, consult: www.DictionaryofSpiritualTerms.com.
This on-line Dictionary of Spiritual Terms provides extensive definitions, examples and related terms in other languages.

# Titles on Christianity by World Wisdom

*Chartres and the Birth of the Cathedral, Revised,*
by Titus Burckhardt, 2009

*Christian Spirit,*
edited by Judith Fitzgerald and Michael Oren Fitzgerald, 2004

*A Christian Woman's Secret: A Modern-Day Journey to God,*
by Lilian Staveley, 2009

*Christianity/Islam: Perspectives on Esoteric Ecumenism*
*A New Translation with Selected Letters,*
by Frithjof Schuon, 2008

*The Destruction of the Christian Tradition: Updated and Revised,*
by Rama P. Coomaraswamy, 2006

*For God's Greater Glory: Gems of Jesuit Spirituality,*
edited by Jean-Pierre Lafouge, 2006

*The Foundations of Christian Art: Illustrated,*
by Titus Burckhardt, 2006

*The Fullness of God: Frithjof Schuon on Christianity,*
selected and edited by James S. Cutsinger, 2004

*In the Heart of the Desert, Revised:*
*The Spirituality of the Desert Fathers and Mothers,*
by John Chryssavgis, 2008

*Men of a Single Book:*
*Fundamentalism in Islam, Christianity, and Modern Thought,*
by Mateus Soares de Azevedo, 2010

*Messenger of the Heart: The Book of Angelus Silesius,*
by Angelus Silesius, 2005

*Not of This World: A Treasury of Christian Mysticism,*
compiled and edited by James S. Cutsinger, 2003

*Paths to the Heart: Sufism and the Christian East,*
edited by James S. Cutsinger, 2002

*Paths to Transcendence:*
*According to Shankara, Ibn Arabi & Meister Eckhart,*
by Reza Shah-Kazemi, 2006

*The Quiet Way: A Christian Path to Inner Peace,*
by Gerhard Tersteegen, 2008

*The Sermon of All Creation: Christians on Nature,*
edited by Judith Fitzgerald and Michael Oren Fitzgerald, 2005

*Shakespeare's Sonnets and the Bible:*
*A Spiritual Interpretation with Christian Sources,*
by Ira Zinman, 2009

*Siena, City of the Virgin: Illustrated,*
by Titus Burckhardt, 2008

*Ye Shall Know the Truth: Christianity and the Perennial Philosophy,*
edited by Mateus Soares de Azevedo, 2005